STARS
AND PLANETS

Suvina Jayatilaka
8.5.92.

STARS AND PLANETS

ROBIN KERROD

Illustrated by
Ron Jobson

Consultants
Bryan Foster and James Muirden

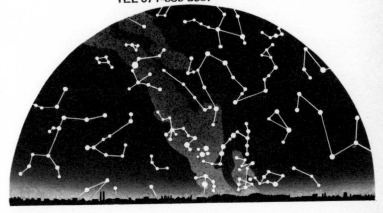

RAINBOW
·BOOKS·

This edition published in 1991 by Rainbow Books,
Elsley House, 24–30 Great Titchfield Street,
London W1P 7AD

Originally published in 1979 by Kingfisher Books

ISBN 1 871745 36 5

Printed and bound in Italy

CONTENTS

INTRODUCTION

Astronomy can with some justification claim to be the oldest science – the first systematic study of something. It grew up as Man was taking his first hesitant steps towards civilization, forsaking the nomadic life of the hunter and gatherer for the more settled existence of the farmer. In the regular rhythm of the heavens, he perceived a means of marking the passage of time. The establishment of an accurate calendar became essential so that Man could regulate the sowing, planting and harvesting of his crops, the timing of his religious festivals and the thousand and one other activities of a community existence.

Millennia before Christ, the Chaldeans, the Babylonians and ancient Egyptians were skilled observers of the heavens. So were the ancient Europeans. It has only been recently appreciated that early European Man, although apparently living a caveman existence, was at least as skilled and if anything more skilled in astronomy than his contemporaries in the Middle East. The megalithic monuments of north-western Europe – the great henges and lines like those at Stonehenge and Carnac – were their observatories, and they were laid out with astonishing precision.

Whereas the megalithic astronomers had to rely on their eyes alone, twentieth century astronomers are blessed with sophisticated instruments of many kinds. Not only can they look at the heavens in visible light, but they can study the wavelengths in the invisible spectrum, from X-ray to radio waves. They also send their instruments into space where viewing is unhampered by the Earth's atmosphere.

Their instruments reveal a universe that is more baffling year by year – a universe populated not only by ordinary stars and galaxies, but by star-like bodies as bright as galaxies; by black holes that swallow up matter like cosmic vacuum cleaners; by bursters, pulsars, and a host of other mysterious bodies. The truth of J.B.S. Haldane's remark that 'the universe is queerer than we *can* imagine' is becoming ever more apparent.

In the wake of such discoveries, has astronomy as practised by the amateur lost its appeal? Not at all. Even to the naked eye, the night sky remains endlessly fascinating as the Moon, the planets, meteors and comets move against the velvety backcloth of space. Through binoculars and telescope, a multitude of other heavenly bodies spring into view – rich star clusters and flaming nebulae, coloured double stars, and far-off galaxies whose light has been travelling for millions of years.

Left: The Trifid nebula in Sagittarius.

Inset left: Stonehenge, England

Key Dates

BC

c. 4000 Chinese record eclipses.
c. 3000 Babylonian and Egyptian astronomy develops.
c. 2000 Stonehenge is established as astronomical observatory.
6th cent. Thales of Miletus, the first great Greek philosopher, considers the Earth is round. He is believed to have predicted the 585 BC solar eclipse. Pythagoras or his followers develop a cosmology in which the Earth and other heavenly bodies circle around a central fire. They believe that contemplating the motion of heavenly bodies holds the key to the harmony of the universe.
5th cent. Meton of Athens works out the 19-year Metonic cycle, after which the Moon's phases are repeated on the same days of the month.
4th cent. Greek astronomer Eudoxus of Cnidus develops a model of the universe in which the circular movement of concentric spheres represents the motion of heavenly bodies around Earth. Heracleides of Pontus considers that the Earth spins on its axis.
3rd cent. Aristarchus of Samos proposes that the Earth moves around the Sun. Eratosthenes measures the size of the Earth and compiles a star catalogue.
2nd cent. Hipparchus compiles his catalogue of over 1000 stars. He discovers the precession of the equinoxes.

AD

2nd cent. Ptolemy of Alexandria builds on the astronomy of the ancient Greeks, particularly Hipparchus. In a great encyclopedic work, he develops detailed theories of the motion of heavenly bodies using a system of deferents and epicycles elaborated by Hipparchus and even earlier by Apollonius.
827 Ptolemy's astronomical encyclopedia is translated into Arabic as the *Almagest* ('The Greatest'), and accelerates growth of Arabian astronomy.
1054 Chinese astronomers witness supernova in Taurus (origin of Crab nebula).
1252 *Alphonsine Tables* are completed in Spain – the best tables of planetary positions yet compiled.

1428 Ulugh Begh founds observatory at Samarkand.
1543 Nicolaus Copernicus publishes *De Revolutionibus Orbium Cœlestium* (*Concerning the Revolution of Celestial Spheres*), in which he proposes a Sun-centred universe.
1576 Tycho Brahe founds Uraniborg Observatory on the island of Hven, Denmark.
1600 Giordano Bruno is burned at the stake for supporting Copernican theory.
1608 Hans Lippershey designs first telescope.
1609 Galileo makes first telescopic observation of heavens. Johannes Kepler publishes first two laws of planetary motion.
1619 Kepler publishes his third law.
1627 Kepler publishes the *Rudolphine Tables* of planetary positions, which supersedes the *Alphonsine Tables*.
1632 Galileo publishes *Dialogue*, supporting a Copernican view of the universe, which leads within a year to his appearance before the Inquisition for heresy.
1666 Isaac Newton formulates his laws of gravity.
1668 Newton builds first reflecting telescope.

1675 Greenwich Observatory is founded. Rømer measures speed of light.
1687 Newton publishes the *Principia*, announcing the laws of gravity and motion.

1705 Edmond Halley predicts the return (in 1758) of the comet now named after him.

1767 Nevil Maskelyne founds the *Nautical Almanac*, which lists positions of the heavenly bodies for every day of the year.

1781 Charles Messier publishes his catalogue of nebulae and star clusters. William Herschel discovers Uranus.

1783 Goodricke explained the variability of the star Algol.

1801 Giuseppe Piazzi discovers Ceres, the largest asteroid.

1802 Herschel discovers binary stars. William Hyde Wollaston observes dark adsorption lines in Sun's spectrum.

1814 Joseph Fraunhofer investigates lines in solar spectrum, now named after him.

1838 Friedrich Wilhelm Bessel determines first stellar parallax and hence measures distance to first star – 61 Cygni.

1842 Christian Doppler explains the wavelength-change effect now named after him.

1843 Schwabe discovers sunspot cycle.

1846 John Couch Adams and Urbain Leverrier independently predict an eighth planet (Neptune), subsequently discovered by Johann Gottfried Galle.

1859 Gustav Kirchoff explains nature of Fraunhofer lines.

1863 Pietro Angelo Secchi first classifies stars by their spectral type.

1877 Giovanni Schiaparelli observes 'canali' on Mars. Asaph Hall discovers the Martian moons Phobos and Deimos.

1891 George Ellery Hale invents spectroheliograph for photographing the Sun at a single wavelength.

1905 Ejnar Hertzsprung suggests that there are giant and dwarf stars. Albert Einstein announces his General Theory of Relativity which is to revolutionize ideas of space, time and motion.

1912 Henrietta Leavitt discovers the period-luminosity relationship of Cepheids.

1913 Henry Norris Russell announces relationship between stellar luminosity and spectral type.

1916 Einstein publishes his Special Theory of Relativity.

1918 100-inch Hooker telescope completed at Mt Wilson observatory. Vesto Melvin Slipher discovers galactic red shifts, which support the theory of an expanding universe.

1925 Edwin Powell Hubble confirms existence of external galaxies with 100-inch telescope.

1927 Jan Hendrik Oort develops theory for rotation of the Galaxy.

1929 Hubble establishes the distance-velocity relationship for the Galaxy.

1930 Clyde Tombaugh discovers Pluto.

1931 Karl Jansky discovers radio waves from outer space.

1937 Grote Reber builds first radio telescope.

1948 200-inch Hale telescope completed at Palomar Observatory.

1951 Discovery of 21-cm radiation from interstellar hydrogen atoms.

1952 Walter Baade revises distances to the galaxies.

1955 Jodrell Bank radio telescope completed.

1957 Russia launches first artificial satellites – Sputniks 1 and 2.

1959 Russian probe Lunik 3 photographs Moon's hidden side.

1960 Quasars are discovered.

1962 First successful interplanetary probe, Mariner 2, reports on Venus.

1963 Background radiation, apparently from the Big Bang, discovered.

1965 Mariner 4 takes close-ups of Mars.

1967 Cambridge astronomers discover pulsars. Venera 4 probe lands on Venus.

1969–1972 Manned Moon landings.

1973 Pioneer 10 probe investigates Jupiter. US launches Skylab.

1976 Viking probes land on Mars.

1977 The rings of Uranus are discovered.

1979 Voyagers 1 and 2 pass Jupiter and head for Saturn encounters in 1980 and 1981. Voyager 2 passes Uranus in 1986 and Neptune in 1989.

1981 The first Space Shuttle *(Columbia)* launched.

1985 Russian Vega probes examine Venus.

1986 Voyager 2 reaches Uranus. Discovers 10 new moons. Halley's Comet explored by space probe Giotto. Launch of Soviet space station Mir. Space Shuttle *Challenger* explodes.

1987 The brightest supernova for four centuries observed in the Large Magellanic Cloud.

1990 Space Telescope launched.

Patterns in the Sky

At first sight, the night sky presents a confusing image of thousands of stars dotted haphazardly against a black backcloth. On closer acquaintance, however, we observe that many of the bright stars form easily recognizable patterns, which do not change over the years. It is by means of these star patterns, or constellations, that astronomers find their way through the heavens.

Early astronomers recognized the usefulness of the constellations, and the names of many constellations date from several centuries before Christ. The constellations are known both by their Latin names and their English equivalents. Easily recognizable constellations include: Ursa Major, the Great Bear; Cassiopeia; Cygnus, the Swan; Leo, the Lion; Orion; Scorpius, the Scorpion; Crux, the Southern Cross; Sagittarius, the Archer.

The names of the constellations are supposed to reflect the shapes that the stars appear to make. But only in a few cases (eg Scorpius, Cygnus) does this hold. It would require a stretch of the imagination to discern the shape of a bull in the pattern of stars in Taurus, or the shape of twin boys in the Gemini constellation. The ancients, however, were highly imaginative. They imagined they saw in the heavens mythological creatures (centaur, unicorn, sea goat); heroes, kings and queens (the mighty hunter Orion, King Cepheus, Queen Cassiopeia); animals galore, as we have already noted; and everyday objects (cup, scales, arrow).

The ancients thought that the stars were fixed on the inside of a great dark globe that surrounded and circled around the Earth. They regarded the Earth as the fixed centre of the universe. We now know otherwise, but this simple concept of a celestial sphere provides a useful model even today, because we do appear to be at the centre of a hollow star-studded sphere that spins around the Earth once a day. And we can identify the positions of heavenly bodies in relation to that sphere. Basic features of the celestial sphere are the celestial poles, which lie directly above the Earth's geographical poles; and the celestial equator, which is the projection of the Earth's equator on to the celestial sphere.

Astronomers at Istanbul Observatory during the Middle Ages used a variety of instruments.

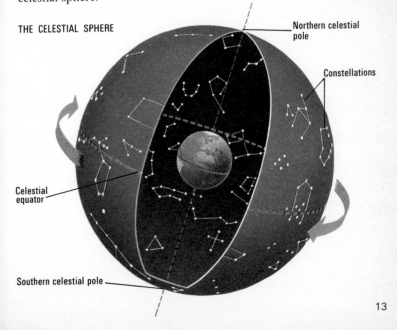

THE CELESTIAL SPHERE

Northern celestial pole

Constellations

Celestial equator

Southern celestial pole

THE CONSTELLATIONS

1 Andromeda
2 Antlia, *Air Pump*
3 Apus, *Bird of Paradise*
4 Aquarius, *Water-Bearer*
5 Aquila, *Eagle*
6 Ara, *Altar*
7 Aries, *Ram*
8 Auriga, *Charioteer*
9 Boötes, *Herdsman*
10 Caelum, *Chisel*
11 Camelopardis, *Giraffe*
12 Cancer, *Crab*
13 Canes, Venatici, *Hunting Dogs*
14 Canis Major, *Great Dog*

15 Canis Minor, *Little Dog*
16 Capricornus, *Sea Goat*
17 Carina, *Keel*
18 Cassiopeia
19 Centaurus, *Centaur*
20 Cepheus
21 Cetus, *Whale*
22 Chamaeleon
23 Circinus, *Compasses*
24 Columba, *Dove*
25 Coma Berenices, *Berenice's Hair*
26 Corona Austrinus, *Southern Crown*

27 Corona Borealis, *Northern Crown*
28 Corvus, *Crow*
29 Crater, *Cup*
30 Crux, *Southern Cross*
31 Cygnus, *Swan*
32 Delphinus, *Dolphin*
33 Dorado, *Swordfish*
34 Draco, *Dragon*
35 Equuleus, *Colt*
36 Eridanus
37 Fornax, *Furnace*
38 Gemini, *Twins*
39 Grus, *Crane*
40 Hercules
41 Horologium, *Clock*
42 Hydra, *Water Serpent*

NORTHERN HEMISPHERE

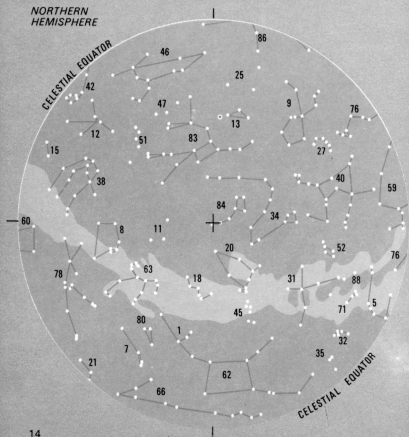

SOUTHERN HEMISPHERE

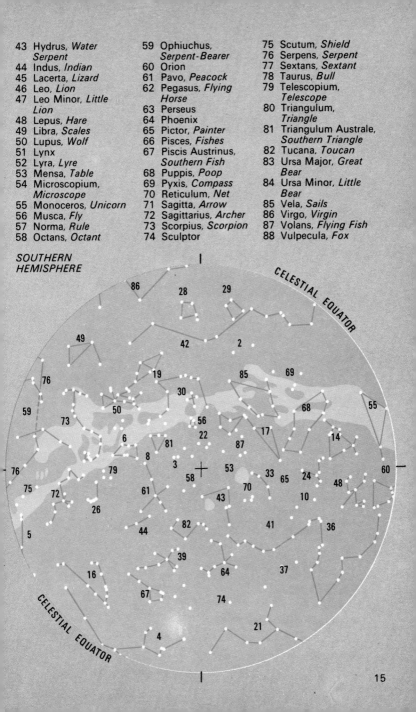

15

The Changing Seasons

If you look at the night sky in the same direction at the same time of night over a period of months, you notice that different constellations come into view.

Let us assume, for example, that you are looking south, in the northern hemisphere, at midnight. In January, depending exactly where you are, you might see the constellations shown above. In July, though, you would see the constellations shown below. They are completely different. In a similar way an observer looking north in the southern hemisphere would see different constellations in January (top right) and those below in July (bottom right).

The reason why the constellations are different becomes obvious from the diagrams (right). The Earth circles around the Sun once a year.

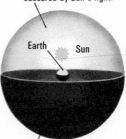

JANUARY
Stars in this part obscured by Sun's light.

Earth   Sun

Stars visible in this part of celestial sphere.

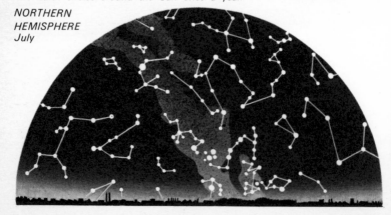

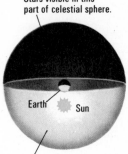

JULY

Stars visible in this part of celestial sphere.

Earth   Sun

Stars in this part obscured by Sun's light.

When the Earth is on one side of the Sun, say in January, only the stars in that part of the celestial sphere away from the Sun can be seen, for that is when it is Earth night. The stars in the celestial sphere beyond the Sun cannot be seen because it is daylight.

Six months later, in July, the situation is reversed; the Earth has travelled in its orbit to the other side of the Sun. The part of the celestial sphere that was previously visible at night is now obliterated by the light from the Sun. And the part that previously lay beyond the Sun is now visible during Earth night.

The seasonal changes in the constellations you see looking north in the northern hemisphere and looking south in the southern hemisphere are not so marked. This is because some of the constellations are circumpolar — they describe a circle around the north or south celestial pole without ever disappearing from view.

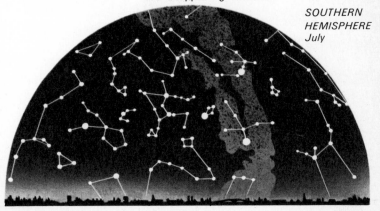

17

The Whirling Heavens

Because the Earth is spinning on its axis, the celestial sphere appears to rotate. It is this diurnal rotation that makes the stars, the Sun, and other heavenly bodies rise and set daily. Since the Earth spins from west to east, the heavenly bodies appear to travel in the opposite direction, rising in the east and setting in the west.

The movement of the stars varies according to where you are on the Earth's surface and in which direction you look. If you are at the north or south pole looking overhead, the stars describe circles around the celestial pole. They remain parallel with the horizon (diagram 1, page 20). As you move into mid-latitudes, the celestial poles are somewhere between the horizon and the zenith (point above the observer). Looking north in the northern hemisphere, for example, the stars move as shown in diagram 2.

Looking south, on the other hand, a star describes an arc travelling from east to west (diagram 3). They culminate, or reach their highest point, on the meridian – the great north-south circle around the celestial sphere (see below). On the equator the celestial poles lie on the horizon and the stars rise and set vertically (diagram 4).

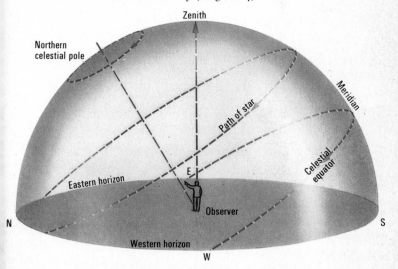

ASPECTS OF THE CELESTIAL SPHERE

An observer's view of the heavens is bounded by the *horizon*, the great circle that marks where the observer's horizontal plane meets the celestial sphere. The point on the sphere directly above him is the *zenith*. The point on the sphere diametrically opposite the zenith, beneath the observer, is the *nadir*. The great circle through the zenith and the celestial poles is the *meridian*. Looking south, stars reach their highest altitude on the meridian. The paths of the stars are parallel to the *celestial equator*, the plane of which is inclined at an angle to the horizon except at the poles. The altitude of the celestial pole is the same as the latitude.

◄ *A long-exposure photograph of the night sky showing the apparent motion of the stars around the north celestial pole.*

The diurnal rotation makes life difficult for the telescopic observer, for the stars in his viewfinder are changing position all the time. They change both in altitude (height above the horizon) and azimuth (distance horizontally). Telescopes are therefore usually mounted so that they can readily follow the path of the stars (see page 117).

Diagram 1

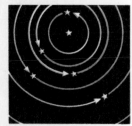

Diagram 2

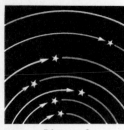

Diagram 3

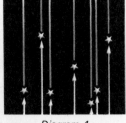

Diagram 4

Star Time

The diurnal rotation provides the basis for our time. Our clocks are set according to solar time, the solar day of 24 hours being the period it takes for the Earth to spin once on its axis *relative to the Sun*.

But the Earth itself has moved relative to the Sun during this time as it journeys in its orbit, and *relative to the stars* it has completed more than one revolution on its own axis. The Earth actually revolves once relative to the stars in 23 hours 56 minutes – four minutes less than the solar day. (See diagram below).

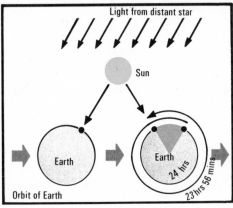

Light from distant star

Sun

Earth

Earth
24 hrs

Orbit of Earth

23 hrs 56 mins

This means that, according to ordinary (solar) time, the stars rise, culminate and set four minutes earlier every day. This amounts to about two hours a month and 24 hours a year.

According to solar time, the stars rise, culminate and set at a given hour only once a year, on or near the same date. That is when the Earth has returned to the same point in its orbit around the Sun.

Things become much simpler, from an astronomical point of view, if we define time

Left: The way you see the stars move depends on where you are and where you look.

in terms of the true period of the Earth's rotation, that is, *relative to the stars*. We call this period a sidereal day and split it into 24 sidereal hours. Then, according to sidereal time, the stars will rise, culminate and set at the same hour every day. In other words, we can relate the position of the stars to sidereal time. This is fundamental to positional astronomy.

Any method of time measurement requires a starting point. For solar time it is Greenwich Mean Time (GMT) – the time at the meridian at Greenwich, the zero meridian of longitude. For sidereal time, the starting point is the First Point of Aries. It is one of the two points on the celestial sphere where the plane of the celestial equator cuts the plane of the ecliptic (see below). Sidereal time is the number of sidereal hours since the First Point of Aries last passed the observer's meridian.

Just as ordinary time differs for places at different longitudes, so does sidereal time. To aid observers, astronomical almanacs incorporate tables relating sidereal time and solar time at intervals throughout the year for a particular location – for example, the Greenwich meridian. To convert Greenwich Sidereal Time (GST) into Local Sidereal Time (LST), for instance, allowance has to be made for the difference in longitude between the observation point and Greenwich. (There is a difference in time of 4 minutes for each degree of longitude east or west of Greenwich. If you are west of Greenwich, you subtract this correction to get Local Sidereal Time, and if you are to the east, you add it.)

THE ECLIPTIC

Observed from Earth, the Sun appears to move in a great circle around the celestial sphere during the year. This great circle is called the ecliptic. The plane of the ecliptic is the plane of the Earth's orbit around the Sun. It makes an angle of $23\frac{1}{2}°$ with the plane of the celestial equator. This is because the Earth's axis is tilted $23\frac{1}{2}°$ in relation to the plane of its orbit around the Sun

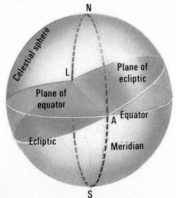

This tilt gives rise to the seasons (page 89).

A band of the sky about 9° on either side of the ecliptic contains the paths of the Moon and most planets and is called the zodiac. The constellations in this band are called zodiacal constellations (page 85).

The Sun passes over the celestial equator twice a year at the time of the equinoxes: when it is travelling north (vernal equinox, about March 21) and south (autumnal equinox about September 23). The planes of the ecliptic and the celestial equator intersect at these times. The point of intersection at the vernal equinox, the First Point of Aries, is the zero point in positional astronomy (see page 22). The point of intersection at the autumnal equinox is the First Point of Libra.

The vernal equinox was in Aries at the time the 'First Point' got its name – over 2000 years ago. But because of precession (page 23), it is now in Pisces, having 'slipped' one whole zodiacal constellation. Similarly, the First Point of Libra is now in Virgo.

Pinpointing the Stars

It is not difficult to locate some of the brightest stars in the sky when they form part of constellations whose shapes are easily recognizable, or when they can be found using other constellations as pointers (see page 24). But many other bright stars and all the fainter ones cannot be so conveniently located. Astronomers therefore require a kind of map reference to pinpoint a star's exact location on the celestial sphere. The most common method of celestial reference is very similar to terrestrial latitude and longitude.

Terrestrial latitude is the angular distance of an object north or south of the Earth's equator. Terrestrial longitude is the angular distance along the equator from the Greenwich meridian to the meridian passing through the object. It is measured east or west of Greenwich.

Celestial latitude, or *declination*, is the angular distance of a star north (positive) or south (negative) of the celestial equator. It is measured in degrees. Celestial longitude, or *right ascension*, is the angular distance along the celestial equator from the First Point of Aries (page 21) to the hour circle through the star (the great circle that passes through the star and the celestial poles). It is measured eastwards from the First Point of Aries in units of sidereal time. We can use these units, since the position of a star on the celestial sphere is a function of time (page 20).

Thus, the brightest star in the sky, Sirius, has co-ordinates: right ascension (RA) 06 hours 43 min, declination (Dec) −16° 39′. The negative declination shows that Sirius is located south of the celestial equator.

The brilliant star Vega, in Lyra, has co-ordinates: RA 18 hours 35 minutes, Dec +38°44′. The positive declination tells us that the star

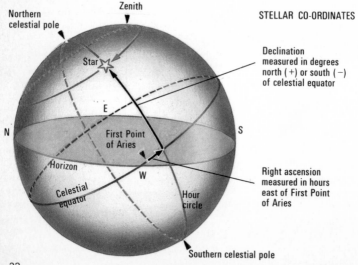

STELLAR CO-ORDINATES

Northern celestial pole

Zenith

Star

Declination
measured in degrees
north (+) or south (−)
of celestial equator

E

N

First Point
of Aries

S

Horizon

W

Celestial
equator

Hour
circle

Right ascension
measured in hours
east of First Point
of Aries

Southern celestial pole

PRECESSION

The positions of the celestial poles and celestial equator do not remain fixed on the celestial sphere. They wander in a predictable way because of the phenomenon of precession. The celestial poles, for example, describe a circle on the celestial sphere, which repeats itself every 25,800 years. Because of precession, the equinoxes are wandering westwards, so that gradually the seasons are changing. The vernal equinox, now in Pisces (March 21), occurs about a month earlier than it did 2000 years ago, when it was in Aries.

Precession results from the gravitational influence of the Sun and Moon on the equatorial bulge of the Earth. A similar effect is observed when a top spins — instead of spinning upright it tends to describe a circle around the vertical.

Because of precession, Polaris will eventually cease to be the pole star. At the time of the building of the Great Pyramid in Egypt, over 4500 years ago, Thuban in Draco was the pole star. The builders lined up one of the pyramid's main passages with it. In about AD 10,000, Deneb in Cygnus will be the pole star; and in AD 14,000 it will be the turn of Vega in Lyra.

Although the precessional period of 25,800 years seems long, the effect of precession must be allowed for in accurate observational astronomy. It is the main factor in the periodic updating of star positions in star catalogues and almanacs.

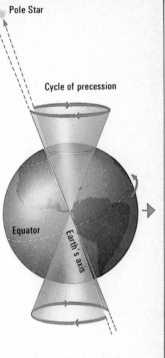

Wobbling like a spinning top, the Earth's axis describes a circle in space every 25,800 years.

is situated in the northern heavens. Polaris, the pole star, is located at RA 01 hours 49 minutes, Dec +89 02′. It is less than one degree removed from the northern celestial pole and its diurnal motion is scarcely discernible.

The co-ordinates of the stars are not completely fixed. Precession (see above) alters the frame of reference. The proper motion of the stars themselves also slowly causes the co-ordinates to change, as do other slight influences. Star positions are therefore updated periodically to allow for this. At present, most star catalogues and charts use the positions of the stars in 1950 as a basis for comparison. 1950 is the so-called standard epoch of observation. The co-ordinates of Sirius, Vega and Polaris given above relate to Epoch 1950. Astronomical atlases often give formulae for working out up-to-date co-ordinates from those of the standard epoch.

KEY CONSTELLATIONS

It is not always easy to translate the constellations shown on small star maps into reality in the vast night sky. But several of the constellations are easily recognisable and it is advisable to use these as signposts to others that are less distinctive. Two of the most prominent constellations in the heavens are Ursa Major – the Great Bear, and Orion. They are useful as pointers to many other stars and constellations, as the diagrams here show.

Ursa Major

This constellation, though close to the north celestial pole, is visible north of latitude 40° south, while it is circumpolar north of latitude 40° north.

Following the handle of the Plough along in a curve we can locate Arcturus (in Boötes), while the four stars in the ploughshare form pointers to Deneb (Cygnus), Vega (Lyra), Castor (Gemini), Capella (Auriga), Regulus (Leo), and perhaps most important Polaris, the pole star. Arcturus and Regulus form a conspicuous triangle with Spica (Virgo) farther south.

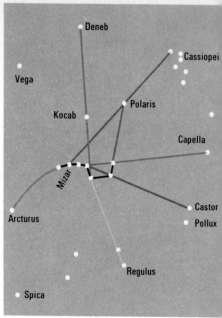

URSA MAJOR

Orion

This magnificent constellation, containing the first magnitude Rigel and Betelgeuse, sits astride the celestial equator and can thus act as a valuable guide to observers in both hemispheres.

The three stars making up Orion's belt point south to the brightest star in the sky, Sirius (Canis Major), north to the orange Aldebaran (Taurus) and the Pleiades cluster, and beyond that to the 'Winking Demon' Algol (Perseus). Procyon (Canis Minor), Castor (Gemini) and Capella (Auriga) can also be readily found.

ORION

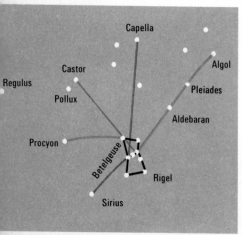

Star Maps

The maps on the following pages show the positions of the stars on the celestial sphere. Like all maps, they slightly distort what they represent, since they show what is a curved surface on flat paper. The maps are criss-crossed with a reference grid which shows the equatorial co-ordinates of right ascension and declination. The co-ordinates relate to Epoch 1950. As the diagram shows, the sky is divided into six equatorial segments and northern and southern circumpolar regions.

Stars are included down to the fourth magnitude of brightness (see page 44). Many of the best-known stars are named. Others that are referred to in the text accompanying the maps are identified by α, β, γ and so on, according to the Bayer system. This classifies the stars in a constellation in order of their brightness, using the Greek alphabet.

Also included on the maps are the brighter star clusters, galactic nebulae and external galaxies. They are identified by their Messier (M) number or by their NGC (New General Catalogue) number.

To find out which stars you are able to see during the year subtract your latitude, say $55°$, from $90°$. This gives $35°$. Then if you are in the northern hemisphere you will be able to see stars south to a declination of $-35°$. Stars with a declination greater than $+35°$ will be circumpolar. If you are in the southern hemisphere, reverse the signs.

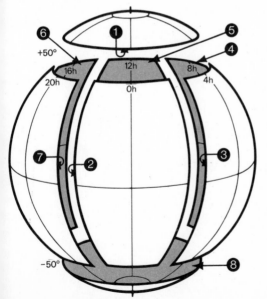

Segmented celestial sphere showing how the star maps that follow relate to it.

1 Circumpolar stars (N)

2 RA 22 hours – 2 hours

3 RA 2 hours – 6 hours

4 RA 6 hours – 10 hours

5 RA 10 hours – 14 hours

6 RA 14 hours – 18 hours

7 RA 18 hours – 22 hours

8 Circumpolar stars (S)

STAR MAP 1 – NORTHERN CIRCUMPOLAR STARS

Ursa Major, the Great Bear (UMa)
The seven brightest stars of this constellation form the Plough, or Big Dipper, the most distinctive pattern of stars in northern skies. The mag 2 Mizar (ζ) forms a beautiful naked-eye double with mag 4 Alcor. But a small telescope reveals that Mizar is itself double, the stars forming a true binary system. And a spectroscope reveals that each of these binary components is itself a binary. Mizar is thus a quadruple star.

Merak (β) and the noticeably yellow Dubhe (α) are known as the Pointers because they point almost exactly to the pole star, Polaris. Close to Merak is M97, one of the largest planetary nebulae in the heavens, visible in powerful binoculars. Binoculars will also show the galaxies M81 and M82, both of about mag 8.

Ursa Minor, the Little Bear (UMi)
Also called the Little Dipper, this constellation has only two bright stars. Polaris (α) is located close to the north celestial pole and appears virtually motionless in the northern sky. It is an optical double with a mag 9 companion. Kocab (β) has a noticeable yellow-orange colour.

Cassiopeia (Cas)
A beautiful constellation on the edge of the Milky Way, Cassiopeia has an unmistakable W-shape and is full of interesting objects. α is a reddish star and forms an optical double with a mag 9 bluish star. γ nearby fluctuates irregularly in brightness. ι is a fine triple star, having a yellow primary with two blue companions. ρ is a naked-eye variable of unknown type.

M52 is an open cluster easily seen in binoculars and at about mag 7 has similar brightness to the loose cluster M103, which lies in a beautiful field. Close to 31 Cassiopeiae is NGC 663, another fine open cluster.

Cepheus (Cep)
Not a conspicuous constellation, Cepheus is best found by using α and β Cassiopeiae as pointers. β is a double, whose mag 3 primary is a spectroscope binary. But one of the most interesting stars is δ, a double star whose primary is a variable of precise period. It typifies the class of variables known as Cepheids. The fainter μ is also variable and is named the garnet star because of its glorious red hue.

Draco, the Dragon (Dra)
A long winding constellation not always easy to make out, it contains some fine binocular doubles. ν is a fine wide pair of white stars of mags 4–5. ψ is a double with yellow and blue components. ε is a true binary system, also yellow and blue. η is a binary too. Thuban (α) is interesting in that it was the pole star at the time the Great Pyramid at Giza was constructed. Precession has now carried the pole to near Polaris. Enclosed by the neck of the dragon is NGC 6543 (37 Draconis), a planetary nebula consisting of a bright oval disc with a central mag 10 star.

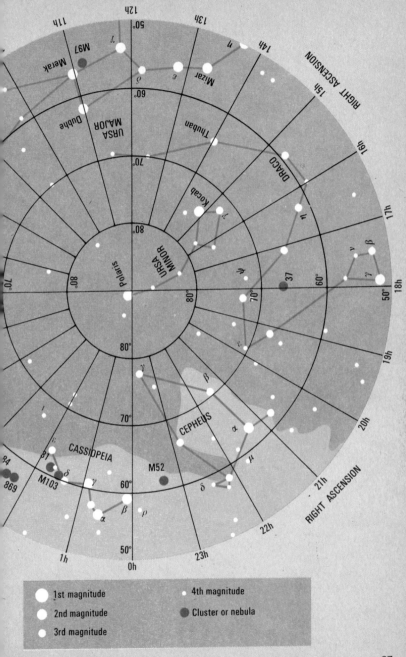

⬤ 1st magnitude	• 4th magnitude
◯ 2nd magnitude	⬤ Cluster or nebula
◦ 3rd magnitude	

27

Pegasus, the Flying Horse (Peg)

An unmistakable constellation, recognized by its prominent square, whose sides go north-south and east-west. Its arrival in the northern skies signifies the approach of northern autumn. The star in the top left-hand corner, however, is shared with Andromeda (α Andromedae). β is a red giant nearly 200 times bigger than the Sun; it is a variable with a period of about 35 days. ζ is a binary, with mag 4 and mag 11 components. In Pegasus too, but on Map 7, is one of the brightest of all globular clusters, M15, which is close by ε Pegasi.

Andromeda (And)

Marked by three bright stars extending from Pegasus, Andromeda is best known for its famous Great Nebula, M31, which is in fact a neighbouring galaxy similar to our own. M31 can be seen with the naked eye as a misty patch, but its spiral form can be made out only on photographs. Close by is a companion galaxy M32. Both belong to the Local Group of galaxies. Other items of interest include α, a mag 2 star with a rich golden colour. γ is a beautiful double, with yellow and blue components.

Triangulum, the Triangle (Tri)

A faint but recognizable constellation south of Andromeda. It contains the galaxy M33, which can be seen in binoculars. M33 belongs to the Local Group of galaxies.

Aries, the Ram (Ari)

An ill-defined zodiacal constellation, whose most interesting star is γ. γ is a fine optical double, with twin mag 4 stars. Close to Hamal (α) is another optical double, λ.

Pisces, the Fishes (Psc)

Another zodiacal constellation astride the ecliptic, Pisces is a faint line of stars south of Andromeda and Pegasus. Because of precession, Pisces now contains the First Point of Aries, which is where the ecliptic crosses the celestial equator. This point marks the vernal equinox, representing the time when the Sun crosses the celestial equator travelling northwards. α is a green and blue double, the brightest of several doubles in the constellation. It serves as a useful pointer for the variable Mira Ceti.

Cetus, the Sea Monster (Cet)

A sprawling constellation, whose most interesting object is o, or Mira. Mira Ceti is an irregular variable that can vary from mag 2 to mag 10 in about a year. Many variables are of the Mira type. Near δ Ceti is the spiral galaxy M77, which is of the Seyfert type (see Map 3).

Aquarius, the Water-Bearer (Aqr)

A large zodiacal constellation close to the celestial equator, containing no really bright stars. ζ is a binary with twin mag 4 components. τ is an optical pair, with a yellow primary of mag 5. ψ is also double. The finest feature of the constellation, however, is the magnificent globular cluster M2, located due north of β near the celestial equator and clearly visible in binoculars (see Map 7).

In this region of the sky, but a little farther south, close to ε, are two other interesting objects. NGC7009 is a planetary nebula named the Saturn Nebula, with faint rays coming from it that resemble Saturn's rings. M72 is another globular cluster.

Piscis Austrinus, the Southern Fish (PsA)

A small constellation prominent because of its white mag 1 star Fomalhaut (α). It can be best located by using α and β Pegasi in the Square of Pegasus as pointers. It lies almost due south of that pair. To the south of Fomalhaut is a line of mag 4 stars extending to the east.

Other Constellations

Grus, the Crane, is easily found but contains little of interest. θ is a binary with mag 4 and mag 7 components. In Phoenix, β is a binary with twin mag 4 components. ζ is an eclipsing variable with a period of a little over $1\frac{1}{2}$ days. Sculptor is undistinguished, containing several faint galaxies and binaries, but they are difficult to locate.

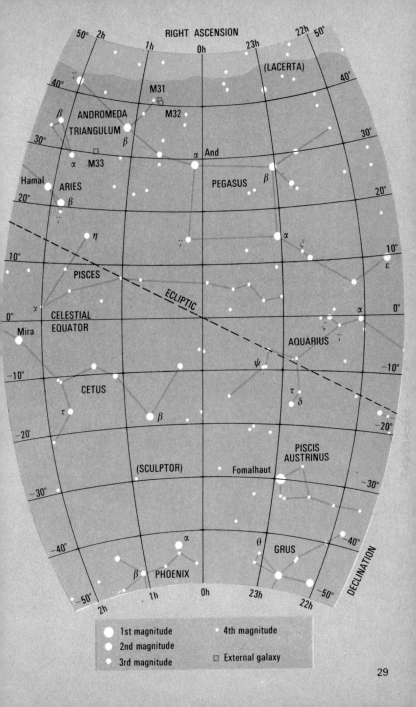

Auriga, the Charioteer (Aur)

This prominent, kite-shaped constellation lies astride the Milky Way and is dominated by the yellow mag 1 Capella (α), sixth brightest star in the heavens. Some 46 light-years away, Capella is physically similar to the Sun. It is a spectroscopic binary. Just south of Capella is a triangle of fainter stars (the Haedi, or Kids), of which ε and ζ are the most interesting. ε is an eclipsing binary with a period of about 27 years. The dim component is one of the most massive stars known, with 20 times the mass of the Sun and a diameter of 290 million km (180 million miles). ζ is also an eclipsing binary, with a period of about $2\frac{1}{2}$ years. θ is an ordinary binary.

Auriga contains three fine star clusters located near the edge of the Milky Way midway between θ Aurigae and β Tauri. Most striking is M37, mag 6 like M36. M38 is a slightly fainter but larger cross-shaped cluster.

Perseus (Per)

Located in the Milky Way between Auriga and Andromeda, Perseus is a constellation rich in star fields. Its most interesting star is Algol (β). Nicknamed the 'Winking Demon', Algol is an eclipsing binary and typifies that class of variable. It dims from mag 2 to mag 3 for a few hours every 2·87 days. Algol is also an optical double. ρ is an irregular variable. η (Map 1) is a double of yellow mag 4 and blue mag 8. ζ and ε are also doubles.

The finest clusters in Perseus are NGC884 and 869, which make up what is called the Sword Handle. Visible to the naked eye, this .double cluster is located midway between α Persei and δ Cassiopeiae. M34 is another naked-eye open cluster.

Taurus, the Bull (Tau)

Arguably the most interesting of the zodiacal constellations, Taurus contains the two fine open clusters, the Pleiades (M45) and the Hyades. The Pleiades is nicknamed the Seven Sisters because most people can identify at least seven of its stars with the naked eye. The Hyades is a more scattered cluster, best seen in binoculars; θ is a naked-eye double.

The Hyades cluster around the bright red star Aldebaran (α), which is not, however, part of the cluster, being much closer (68 light-years) to us. A red giant, Aldebaran is a binary with a faint mag 11 companion. λ is an eclipsing binary of the Algol type with a period of about 4 days. Just north of ζ is the famous Crab Nebula (M1), the still-expanding remnants of the supernova explosion of AD 1054.

Orion (Ori)

A truly magnificent and unmistakable constellation on the celestial equator, depicting the mighty hunter Orion striding across the heavens. Its main outline is made up of two mag 1 and five mag 2 stars. Brilliant white Rigel (β), which is a double, provides a fine contrast with reddish-orange Betelgeuse (α), a red supergiant of truly gigantic dimensions (diameter 400 million km, 250 million miles). Like many red giants it is an irregular variable. Of the three stars in Orion's Belt ζ and δ are doubles. σ is a fine multiple star, as is the magnificent θ, whose four principal components can be seen in a low-power telescope. θ, known as the Trapezium, is immersed in the famous Orion Nebula (M42), the brightest of all nebulae, which is easily visible to the naked eye. This region is referred to as Orion's Sword. Orion provides a very useful means of locating other constellations (see page 24).

Eridanus (Eri)

This long, mainly faint constellation winds its way like the river it is supposed to represent far south from β, near Rigel in Orion, to mag 1 Achernar (α), ninth brightest star in the sky (see Map 8). γ is a noticeably red star; θ is a fine double. ε is interesting because its wobbly motion suggests that it has a planetary system.

Other Constellations

In Lepus, the Hare, β, γ and κ are doubles. R is a faint variable of the Mira type and is interesting because it is one of the reddest stars known. Columba, the Dove, Caelum, the Chisel, and Fornax, the Furnace, contain little of interest.

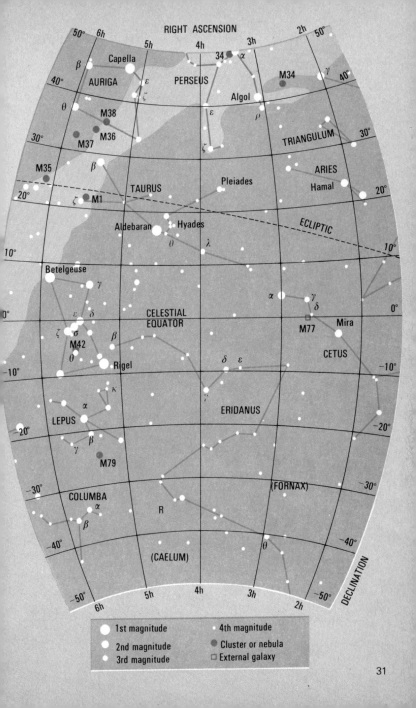

Gemini, the Twins (Gem)

A splendid zodiacal constellation dominated by the twin mag 1 stars Castor (α) and Pollux (β). Castor is a fine binary of pale hue, contrasting with the rich yellow of Pollux. δ is an optical double, as is the reddish μ. κ is a binary, with blue and yellow components. η and ζ are variables varying between mags 3 and 4. η is a semi-regular variable, while ζ is a regular-as-clockwork Cepheid. M35, just beyond η, is one of the clearest open clusters in the sky.

Cancer, the Crab (Cnc)

A faint zodiacal constellation between Leo and Gemini. Most interesting of its features is the fine open cluster M44, called Praesepe, or the Beehive. Easily visible to the naked eye, it appears magnificent in binoculars. ι is a beautiful double, yellow and blue. R, due north of β, is a Mira-type variable with a period of nearly a year, ranging between mags 6 and 11. Close to α is another loose cluster, M67, barely visible to the naked eye.

Canis Minor, the Little Dog (CMi)

Eighth brightest star in the sky Procyon (α) dominates this tiny constellation. Of yellow hue, it is a close optical double with a very faint companion.

Monoceros, the Unicorn (Mon)

A faint constellation lying in the Milky Way, it has no really outstanding stars, but contains some fine clusters. β is a triple star with mag 4 and 5 components.

Roughly midway between β Monocerotis and γ Geminorum is NGC2244, an open cluster around the star 12 Monocerotis which is just visible to the naked eye and exquisite in binoculars. Midway between β and α is the mag 6 cluster M50, while a little beyond α, going in the same direction, is NGC 2506, another rich cluster.

Hydra, the Water Snake (Hya)

A very long constellation that winds itself, serpent-like, through the heavens. The most northerly star, ε, in the 'head' is a double of mags 3 and 6. The only prominent star in the constellation, α, is called Alphard, meaning 'solitary one', because of its seemingly remote position away from other bright stars. M48 is the only prominent star cluster in the group and is just visible to the naked eye, but it is difficult to locate.

Canis Major, the Great Dog (CMa)

The brightest star in the sky, Sirius (α), or the Dog Star, makes this constellation easy to locate. Highly luminous (nearly 30 times more than the Sun) and less than 9 light-years distant, brilliant white Sirius has a mag of $-1 \cdot 45$. It is a binary with a faint white dwarf companion. A little due south of Sirius is the rich cluster M41, scarcely visible to the naked eye.

Puppis, the Poop (Pup)

This constellation represents part of the ship Argo Navis, which in Greek mythology carried Jason on his quest for the Golden Fleece. Vela (Sails) and Carina (Keel) are the other parts of Argo Navis, originally regarded as a single constellation. Puppis spans a rich region of the Milky Way. L² is a variable red star, which varies between about mags 3 and 6 in about $4\frac{1}{2}$ months. Its several double stars include κ, π, σ and h².

The constellation covers a rich region of the heavens and abounds in fine clusters, such as mag 5 M47, which is just visible to the naked eye. Close to it is the rather fainter M46. These can be located a third of the way along a line from Sirius to α Hydrae. Due south of M46 is NGC2440, a bright planetary nebula. Farther south still, near ξ, is the mag 6 cluster M93.

Vela, the Sails (Vel)

A Milky Way constellation rich in star fields and clusters. δ (on Map 8) is a double, as is γ, whose bright component is a variable of a rare class known as WR (for Wolf-Rayet). It is a brilliant blue-white and has a very high surface temperature (nearly 20,000°C). Just south of γ is the cluster NGC2547.

Other Constellations

The southern constellations Antlia, the Airpump, and Pyxis, the Compass, are hard to pinpoint and, like Lynx, contain little of interest.

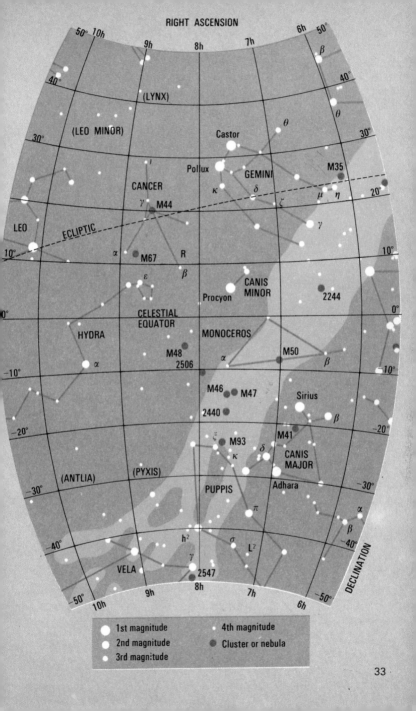

Canes Venatici, the Hunting Dogs (CVn)

A faint constellation which lies beneath the handle of the Plough. Its chief star is α, or Cor Caroli (Charles' Heart), an optical double with mag 3 and 5 components.

Canes Venatici contains many galaxies and clusters. About midway between α and Arcturus in Boötes is a very fine globular cluster, M3, of mag 6. Between β and 20 is the mag 8 spiral galaxy M94. North of 20 lies the fainter spiral M63. Farther north still, near η Ursa Majoris is the famous Whirlpool Galaxy, M51. It is historically interesting as the first galaxy to have its spiral nature observed.

Coma Berenices, Berenice's Hair (Com)

Although this constellation is devoid of any bright stars, it is one of the richest regions of the sky for galaxies and clusters. Indeed, with its neighbour Virgo, it contains the biggest groups of galaxies in the heavens. The largest Coma group has more than 800 members clustered closely together. Most of the galaxies are too faint to be detected in binoculars or in low-power telescopes, but a few are visible. They include M64, a spiral known as the Black-Eye Galaxy, which is mag 6. The spirals M85 and M88 are roughly midway between α Comae and β Leonis. Most prominent of the globular clusters in the constellation is M53, which is close to α and is mag 7.

Leo, the Lion (Leo)

A distinctive zodiacal constellation, and one of the few that does look like its name. Its curved front part looks like a sickle, and is often so called. The southernmost star in the Sickle is mag 1 Regulus (α), which is a double. γ is a fine binary with mag 2 and 3, gold and red components.

Two interesting pairs of galaxies appear in Leo. M65 and M66 are located midway between the binary ι and θ; M66 is somewhat the brighter (mag 8). M95 and M96 can also be found in a similar low-power field and are relatively easy to locate; M96 is the brighter of the two.

Virgo, the Virgin (Vir)

Virgo surpasses even Coma Berenices in the richness of its celestial objects. Its many galaxies are grouped between ε Virginis and β Leonis and are a continuation of the Coma group. The largest cluster of galaxies in Virgo is estimated to contain at least 2500 members. Among the brightest and easiest to find is M58, a barred-spiral galaxy. Close by are the fainter mag 9 elliptical galaxies M59 and M60. M87 is elliptical and of similar brightness. It is a powerful radio source. M49 is also elliptical but somewhat brighter.

Brightest of the stars in this large zodiacal constellation is the blue-white mag 1 Spica (α). γ is a fine binary with components of equal brightness. τ and θ are doubles.

Centaurus, the Centaur (Cen)

One of the most magnificent constellations, Centaurus extends into the far south. Its brightest stars α and β are shown on the circumpolar Map 8. α Centauri, often called Rigil Kent, is the nearest naked-eye star, being only 4·3 light-years away. It is a magnificent and easy binary with a period of 80 years. A mag 11 companion star, Proxima Centauri, is the star nearest to the Sun, at a distance of 4·28 light-years. β Centauri, or Hadar, though apparently near α, is actually a blue giant star some 400 light-years distant. It is a close double. γ, another binary with a period of 85 years, has twin components of mag 3.

Centaurus contains the brightest and finest globular cluster in the heavens, which appears to be a mag 4 star and is designated as ω Centauri. It lies roughly midway between γ and ζ Centauri and is unmistakable. NGC 3766 (Map 8) is another rich cluster, clearly seen in binoculars, which contains more than 200 stars up to mag 8.

Other Constellations

Leo Minor, the Little Lion, Sextans, the Sextant, and Crater, the Cup are small, inconspicuous constellations containing little of interest. Corvus, the Crow, is a compact constellation whose δ is an easy double with a yellow mag 3 primary.

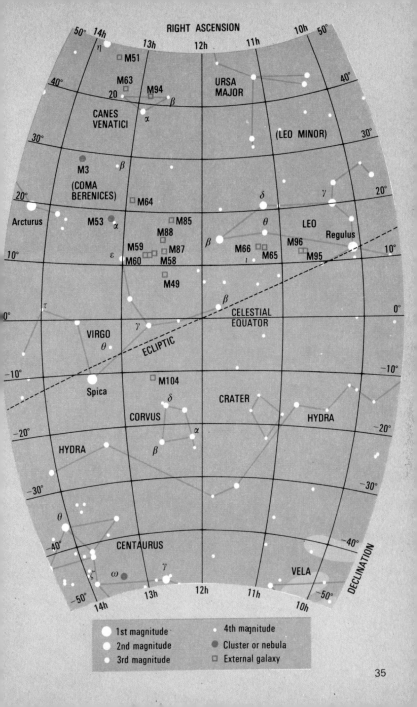

Hercules (Her)

This is a large but not distinctive constellation. α is a red giant irregular variable which changes between mags 3 and 4. κ Ophiuchi in the neighbouring constellation, at about mag 3·5, is a good star to compare it with. α is also a double, with a greenish mag 5 companion. ζ, ρ and μ are binary.

The most interesting feature of Hercules, however, is M13, the finest globular cluster visible in the northern heavens. Just visible to the naked eye between ζ and η, M13 contains hundreds of thousands of stars and lies 25,000 light-years away. The globular cluster M92 is also easily seen in binoculars, being due north of π in an empty part of the sky.

Corona Borealis, the Northern Crown (CrB)

A small but easily recognizable group close to Boötes. It contains several doubles and variables, the most interesting of which are R and T. R is a normally mag 6 star easily found north of δ. At times it dims suddenly to mag 11 or below within a few weeks, and may take years to regain its former brightness. T is an even more fascinating star of a class known as recurrent nova. Normally very faint, it periodically brightens up with nova-like suddenness to mag 2 or 3 and may rival α for a short while.

Boötes, the Herdsman (Boo)

A fine constellation which contains the fourth brightest star in the sky Arcturus (α), a noticeably orange giant of mag −0·2. It is readily found by following the curve of the handle of the Plough southwards. δ is an easy double, seen in binoculars; μ is another wide double. ε is a closer double, with a yellow primary and blue companion of mags 3 and 5 respectively.

Serpens, the Serpent (Ser)

A disjointed constellation separated by Ophiuchus, divided into Caput (Head) and Cauda (Tail). In Serpens Caput, south of Corona Borealis, δ is a close binary. Right at the tip of Serpens Cauda and on Map 7 is θ, an easier double with twin mag 4·5 stars. It lies close to δ Aquilae. The fine globular cluster M5 lies close to 5 Serpentis (mag 5). It is roughly equidistant from α and μ.

Ophiuchus, the Serpent Bearer (Oph)

Although not particularly interesting as far as stars are concerned, this large constellation contains some fine globular clusters, easily visible in binoculars. M10 and M12, both of mag 6·6, are quite readily found in the relatively barren interior of Ophiuchus. The similarly bright M19 and M62 are rather more difficult to find since they lie in the Milky Way, as does the mag 7 M9.

Libra, the Scales (Lib)

This zodiacal constellation is inconspicuous and contains few items of interest. α is a wide double, with a mag 6 companion; ι is also double. The mag 5 δ, easily located close to β, is an eclipsing binary of the Algol type. It has a period of 2·3 days.

Scorpius, the Scorpion (Sco)

A fine constellation, and one of the few that actually resembles its name. It has spreading 'claws' at the head and an arching 'tail'. The most prominent star is the mag 1 Antares (α), a huge red supergiant rivalling Betelgeuse in size and luminosity. Antares is a double, with a greenish companion. β is also double, with a yellow primary and green companion; the primary is a closer double. ν, close to β, is another double, whose components are themselves close doubles.

There are two fine open clusters above the tail of Scorpius, M6 and M7, which at mags 5 and 4 are visible to the naked eye. The globular clusters M4 and M80 are also easily found; M4, close to Antares, and M80 midway between Antares and β Scorpii. They are of mags 6 and 7 respectively.

Lupus, the Wolf (Lup)

A small, bright constellation between Centaurus and Scorpius, Lupus contains little of interest besides the binary η and the open cluster NGC5822, which is close to ε.

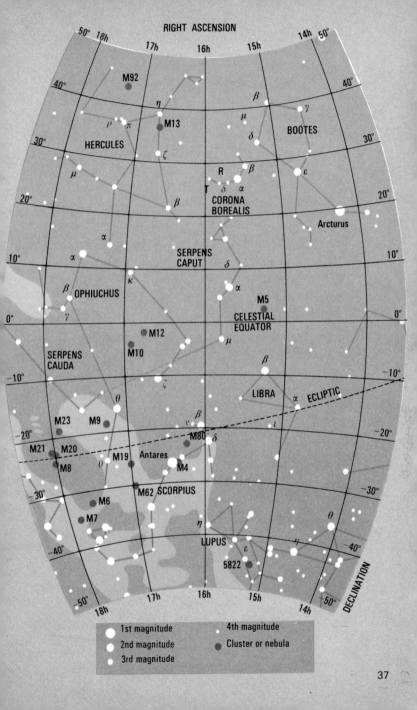

37

Cygnus, the Swan (Cyg)

This prominent constellation, also called the Northern Cross, lies on the Milky Way and contains many fine star fields. The brightest star is mag 1 Deneb (α). Deneb forms one corner of the distinctive Summer Triangle, the other stars being Altair (α Aquilae) and Vega (α Lyrae). The Summer Triangle is a notable feature of the northern summer sky and provides a useful reference base. The constellation's finest star is undoubtedly β, or Albireo, a beautiful double, with rich yellow and greenish-blue components. γ has a faint companion, too, which needs higher power to resolve. δ is a close binary, with mag 3 and mag 6 components and a period of some 300 years. 52 is also binary. χ is a variable star of the Mira type, varying between mags 4 and 14 in 407 days. Close to γ is the peculiar star P, which rose like a nova in 1600 and has remained at mag 5 ever since that time. It is highly luminous. The most easily distinguished star cluster in Cygnus is the large open cluster M39, just inside the Milky Way close to π^2 and ρ.

Lyra, the Lyre (Lyr)

A small, bright constellation dominated by the brilliant blue-white Vega (α), fifth brightest star in the heavens. Close to Vega is the fine naked-eye double ε, both components of which are themselves double. δ is a naked-eye double, too. ζ is an easy low-power double, while β is a double whose primary is the prototype of the bright eclipsing binary. Its variations from mags 3 to 4 can be traced, over a period of about 13 days, by reference to γ (mag 3). Midway between γ and β is the brightest of the planetary nebulae, the Ring Nebula, M57. The globular cluster M56 can be found on a line between γ Lyrae and Albireo.

Aquila, the Eagle (Aql)

Another fine constellation spanning the celestial equator, whose brightest star is Altair (α), mag 0·7. It forms one corner of the Summer Triangle (see Cygnus above). Another interesting star is η, a Cepheid variable with a period of 7·2 days.

Capricornus, the Sea Goat (Cap)

A large zodiacal constellation which is not well-defined. α is an easy naked-eye double, both components of which are themselves double. Of these the primary is an optical pair, while its companion is binary. The fainter component of this binary is itself a binary, but needs quite high power to resolve. β is an easy double for binoculars. M30 is a mag 8 globular cluster found close to ζ.

Sagittarius, the Archer (Sgr)

A beautiful zodiacal constellation, arguably of bow shape, astride the Milky Way. It abounds in interesting features, such as its dense star clouds, which lie in the direction of the centre of our Galaxy. The brightness of the Milky Way in the region and the wealth of features tend to make identification of objects rather difficult. Close to μ is M21 a mag 6 open cluster. Nearby is M20, the famous Trifid Nebula. North of this is the fine open cluster M23. South of M20, is M8, the Lagoon Nebula, just visible to the naked eye. M22, on the edge of the Milky Way, is a large globular cluster easily visible in binoculars. Of mag 6, it contains a number of red stars.

Other Constellations

Vulpecula, the Fox, Sagitta, the Arrow, Delphinus, the Dolphin, and Equuleus, the Little Horse are all small constellations that contain only a few noteworthy features. In Vulpecula, just to the north of γ Sagittae, is M27, a planetary nebula named the Dumbbell. In Delphinus, α and γ are doubles, the latter a yellow and green pair of mags 4 and 5 at the 'nose' of the dolphin. Of the three mag 4 stars of Equuleus, γ is a wide double, easily separated in binoculars.

Scutum, the Shield, is another tiny constellation, and because it straddles the Milky Way it has rich star fields and is a fine region to sweep with binoculars. M11, near β, is a fine open cluster called the Wild Duck. Corona Austrinus, the Southern Crown, is by no means as prominent as its northern counterpart. Microscopium, the Microscope, is inconspicuous.

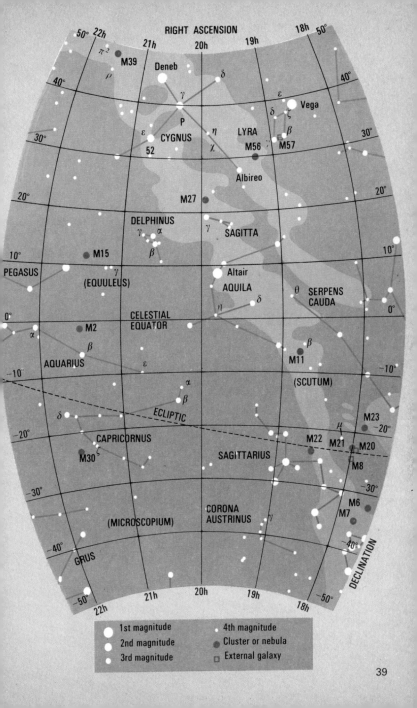

Tucana, the Toucan (Tuc)

A faint group but interesting because it contains most of Nubecula Minor, or the Small Magellanic Cloud, a neighbouring galaxy visible as a dim patch to the naked eye. It also contains two fine globular clusters: one is 47 Tucanae (NGC104), which is visible to the naked eye and the finest such cluster after ω Centauri. NGC362 is the other fine cluster, which is slightly dimmer. β is an easy double, both of whose components are themselves double, though not easily resolved.

Dorado, the Swordfish (Dor)

A faint and dispersed group that contains most of Nubecula Major, or the Large Magellanic Cloud, another neighbouring galaxy. This Cloud is a fine sight in binoculars or a small telescope. It abounds in clusters and nebulae, such as NGC2070, the Looped Nebula, which can be seen even without optical aid. β Doradûs is a Cepheid, with a period of nearly 10 days.

Carina, the Keel (Car)

This large constellation lies south of Vela and extends from Canopus (α), second brightest star in the sky, nearly to Crux, the Southern Cross. Its stars ε and ι make with δ and κ Velae the False Cross, which is sometimes confused with the True Cross. υ is a double with mag 3 and mag 6 components. Directly north of υ is the Cepheid variable l, which ranges from mags 3·5 to 5. Midway on a line joining ι and β is a fine globular cluster, NGC2808. It contains thousands of mag 13–15 stars.

Crux, the Southern Cross (Cru)

The most famous of the southern constellations, Crux, which points nearly to the southern celestial pole, is bounded on three sides by Centaurus (described on page 34). α, or Acrux, is a fine double, easy to resolve. Close to β, on the edge of a 'hole' in the Milky Way, is κ. κ is a spectacular sight, being a red star surrounded by stars of different hues. It is aptly named the Jewel Box. The 'hole' is actually an obscuring dark nebula known as the Coal Sack.

Pavo, the Peacock (Pav)

Quite a large constellation in which κ is most noteworthy. It is one of a class of Cepheids called W Virginis, with a brightness varying between mags 4 and 5 in a little over 9 days. ε is a double. NGC6752 is a large globular cluster, magnificent in binoculars.

Other Constellations

Ara, the Altar, and Triangulum Australe, the Southern Triangle, are close to Pavo and are quite conspicuous, but they contain little of interest. Triangulum Australe contains a fine open cluster of quite bright stars, NGC6025, resolvable in binoculars. Musca, the Fly, and Norma, the Rule, also contain some good clusters. Most of the other southern constellations, however, are unremarkable.

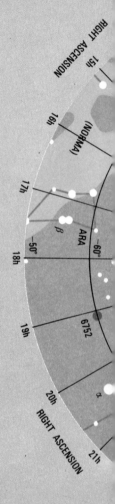

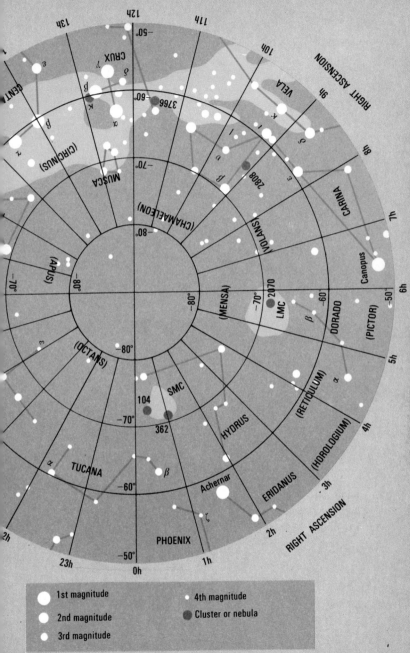

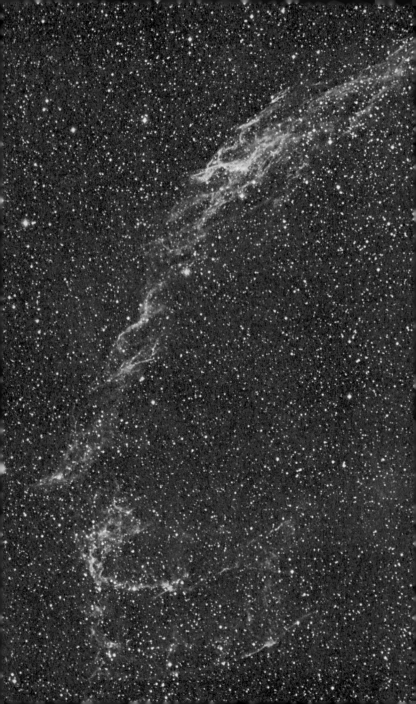

Understanding the Stars

In the main, stars are bodies much like the Sun (see page 108). They are hot gaseous globes that derive the energy they radiate from nuclear fusion reactions within their cores. Even a casual glance at the night sky reveals that the stars are not all alike. Most noticeably, they differ in brightness and colour. The brightest of them form the patterns we know as the constellations, the means by which we find our way through the heavens.

The stars in the constellations seem to be grouped together in space and remain fixed in their positions from century to century. But this is far from the truth. With very few exceptions, the stars in the constellations lie at vastly different distances from us and only happen to be grouped together in the line of sight. And their positions are not fixed either. They are travelling through space at amazing speeds. Their motion is imperceptible only because they are so very far away.

Stellar Distances

It is difficult to imagine how far away the stars are. Stellar distances are so great that they must be expressed, not in terrestrial units such as the mile or kilometre, but in light-years – the distance light travels in a year (about 10 million million kilometres or 6 million million miles). On this scale the nearest star, Proxima Centauri, lies a little over 4 light-years away. The Sun and all the other stars in the sky belong to a star island, or galaxy, that measures about 100,000 light-years across. Other galaxies have been discovered that lie thousands of millions of light-years away. This gives an idea of the enormity of the universe.

Estimating the distance to the stars is one of the astronomer's most difficult tasks. He can calculate distance directly only for a few nearby stars, using the method of parallax illustrated below. This method depends on the fact that a nearby object appears to move against a distant background when viewed from different points. To estimate stellar parallax, the star is viewed from opposite sides of the Earth's orbit (A and B). And the star appears to change position (P_A to P_B). From this change in position, or annual parallax, the distance between the stars and the Earth can be simply calculated.

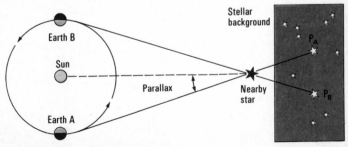

◀ The Veil nebula in Cygnus.

THE NEAREST STARS

Star	RA h m	Dec ° '	Magnitude App	Magnitude Abs	Spectral type	Distance (l-y)
Proxima Centauri	14 26	−62 28	11·1	15·5	M5	4·28
α Centauri A	14 36	−60 38	−0·01	4·4	G2	4·3
B			1·3	5·7	K5	4·3
Barnard's star	17 55	04 24	9·5	13·3	M5	5·9
Wolf 359	10 54	07 20	13·5	16·7	M8	7·6
Lalande 21185	11 01	36 18	7·5	10·5	M2	8·1
Sirius A	06 43	−16 39	−1·45	1·41	A1	8·8
B			8·7	11·6	wA	8·8
UV Ceti A	01 36	−18 13	12·5	15·3	M5	8·9
B			13·0	15·8	M6	8·9
Ross 154	18 47	−23 53	10·6	13·3	M4	9·5
Ross 248	23 40	43 56	12·3	14·8	M6	10·3
ε Eridani	03 31	−09 38	3·7	6·1	K2	10·8
L 789−6	22 36	−15 36	12·2	14·6	M7	10·8
Ross 128	11 45	01 06	11·1	13·5	M5	10·8
61 Cygni A	21 05	38 30	5·2	7·6	K5	11·1
B			6·0	8·4	K7	11·1
Procyon A	07 37	05 21	0·4	2·6	F5	11·4
B			10·7	13·0	wF	11·4
ε Indi	22 00	−57 00	4·7	7·0	K5	11·4

Only a few hundred stars show appreciable parallax, so for the majority of stars indirect methods of calculating distance must be used.

Star Brightness

We measure star brightness on a scale of magnitude derived from one first adopted by ancient Greek astronomers. On this scale the stars visible to the naked eye are divided into six categories of brightness – denoted 1st, 2nd, 3rd, 4th, 5th and 6th magnitudes. The brightest stars in the sky are of 1st magnitude; those just visible, of the 6th. A star of 1st magnitude (mag 1) is $2\frac{1}{2}$ times brighter than one of mag 2, which is $2\frac{1}{2}$ times brighter than one of mag 3, and so on. A mag 1 star is 100 times brighter than a mag 6 star.

To describe the exceptionally bright stars, the scale is extended backwards beyond 1, to 0 and even to negative values. The brightest star in the sky, Sirius, is mag −1·45. In a similar way, the scale is extended beyond 6 to describe stars which are too faint for the naked eye to see,

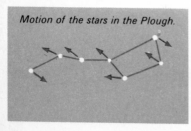

Motion of the stars in the Plough.

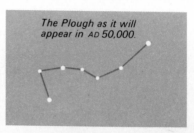

The Plough as it will appear in AD 50,000.

but which are visible in binoculars and telescopes. The largest telescopes can detect stars fainter than mag 20. Data about the 25 brightest stars in the heavens are given on page 48.

The brightness we observe bears little relation to the star's true brightness, of course, because the stars lie at different distances from us. A nearby star will appear brighter than a distant one of the same magnitude. We therefore define an absolute magnitude, which is the magnitude of a star when viewed at a standard distance (33 light-years or 10 parsecs). Thus from an absolute point of view Rigel and Deneb (abs mag -7) far outshine apparently brighter stars like Sirius and Alpha Centauri.

Stellar Motions

Though the stars do move through the heavens, only a few of the nearest ones can be observed to do so. The motion of a star can be resolved into two components, one in the line of sight and one across the line of sight. The latter shows up as a continuing change in the star's position – it is called proper motion. Barnard's star has the largest proper motion, of 10 seconds of arc per year.

The motion in the line of sight (radial motion) – directly towards or away from us – can be determined by studying the spectrum of the light the star gives out (see below). The lines in the spectrum are shifted towards the blue end of the spectrum if the star is approaching us, or towards the red end if the star is receding.

Exploiting the Spectrum

The spectrum of starlight yields a wealth of other information about the emitting star. The degree of widening of the spectral lines, for example, is a measure of the star's rotation velocity on its axis. Splitting of the spectral lines indicates a powerful magnetic field. The relative positions

---

THE STELLAR SPECTRUM

Astronomers discover most information about a star from its light. When passed through a spectroscope, the light is split into a spectrum, or rainbow-like band of colour. The spectrum is marked at intervals with thin black bands, or spectral lines. From the relative position and nature of these lines astronomers can deduce an enormous amount of information.

The dark-line spectrum is produced in the following way. The glowing gases in the star's interior, which are under very great pressure, give off white light. This alone would yield a continuous, or unbroken spectrum. But when this light passes through the star's cooler outer atmosphere, certain wavelengths in it are absorbed. This produces the dark lines. Where the lines appear depends on the chemical elements in the outer atmosphere.

Spectral lines

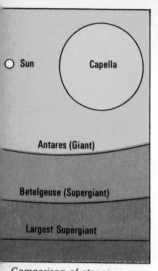

Comparison of star sizes.

Spectra of the Hyades.

of the lines reveal the chemical composition of the star's atmosphere.

The surface temperature of the star can be determined from the distribution of energy in the star's spectrum. Temperatures are found to vary from more than 20,000°C for blue-white stars like Spica to less than 3000°C for red dwarf stars like Proxima Centauri. The intensity of certain spectral lines is a measure of the star's absolute magnitude, or luminosity.

When temperature and luminosity are known, the diameter of the star can be simply calculated, brightness being dependent on surface area as well as on temperature. Stellar diameters vary enormously – from hundreds of millions of kilometres for supergiant stars like Betelgeuse to a mere few thousand kilometres for white dwarfs like the companion of Sirius.

The spectroscopic determination of luminosity (true brightness) also enables the distance to the star to be determined. Brightness decreases as the distance increases, by the inverse square law – at twice the distance, it is a quarter as bright. Thus distance can be calculated by comparing the observed, apparent brightness of a star with its true brightness.

The mass of a star can also be inferred from its luminosity, since the two are related – the greater the mass of a star, the more luminous it is. When a star forms part of a binary-star system (page 50), however, its mass can be found directly. It can be calculated from knowledge of the orbital period of the pair and their distance apart.

Stars do not vary enormously in mass – from about one-tenth to about 10 times the mass of the Sun. But stellar diameters, and hence volumes, vary a great deal. Stellar densities, therefore, vary considerably too – from about one-hundred thousandth the density of water for supergiants to more than a hundred thousand times its density for white dwarfs. Neutron stars have an even greater density (see page 119).

THE HERTZSPRUNG-RUSSELL DIAGRAM

Two inimitable characteristics of a star are its luminosity (absolute magnitude) and its spectrum. Stars can be divided into 10 main classes by virtue of certain features in their spectra, designated O, B, A, F, G, K, M, R, N and S. These classes, which run from high to low surface temperatures, are further divided into 10 sub-classes, 0 to 9.

When spectral class is plotted against luminosity, the stars nearly all fall into fairly distinct groups. This can be seen from the diagram, called the Hertzsprung-Russell diagram after its originators. Most stars, including the Sun, lie in a band called the Main Sequence.

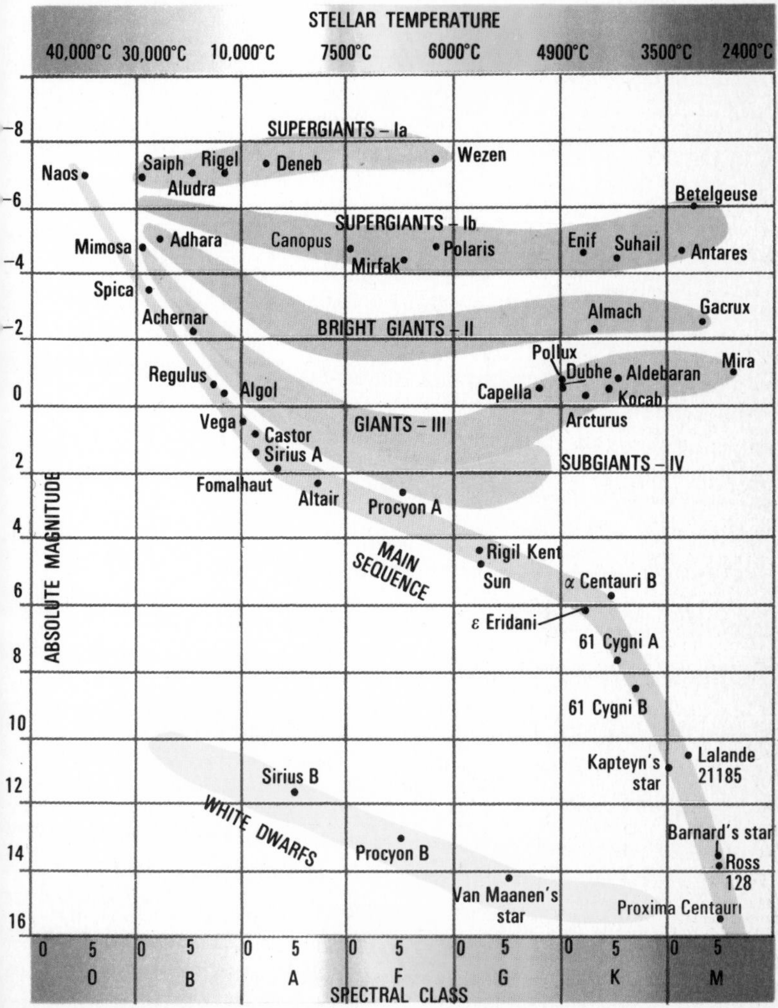

STELLAR TEMPERATURE

40,000°C 30,000°C 10,000°C 7500°C 6000°C 4900°C 3500°C 2400°C

ABSOLUTE MAGNITUDE

-8

SUPERGIANTS – Ia

-6 Naos · Saiph · Rigel · Deneb · Wezen · Betelgeuse
Aludra

-4 Mimosa · Adhara · Canopus SUPERGIANTS – Ib · Enif Suhail · Antares
Mirfak · Polaris

-2 Spica · Achernar BRIGHT GIANTS – II Almach Gacrux

0 Regulus · Algol Pollux Mira
Vega · Castor Capella · Dubhe · Aldebaran
Sirius A Kocab

2 Fomalhaut GIANTS – III Arcturus
Altair SUBGIANTS – IV

4 Procyon A

6 MAIN SEQUENCE · Rigil Kent
Sun α Centauri B

8 ε Eridani 61 Cygni A

10 61 Cygni B

12 Sirius B Kapteyn's star · Lalande 21185

14 WHITE DWARFS Procyon B Barnard's star · Ross 128

16 Van Maanen's star Proxima Centauri

0 5 0 5 0 5 0 5 0 5 0 5 0 5
O B A F G K M

SPECTRAL CLASS

47

THE BRIGHTEST STARS

Star		RA h m	Dec ° '	Magnitude App	Magnitude Abs	Spectral type	Distance (l-y)
Sirius	α CMa	06 43	−16 39	−1·45	1·41	A1	8·8
Canopus	α Car	06 23	−52 40	−0·73	−4·7	F0	196
Rigil Kent	α Cen	14 36	−60 38	−0·2	4·3	G2	4·3
Arcturus	α Boo	14 13	19 26	−0·06	−0·2	K2	36
Vega	α Lyr	18 35	38 44	0·04	0·5	A0	26
Capella	α Aur	05 13	45 57	0·08	−0·6	G8	46
Rigel	β Ori	05 12	−08 15	0·11	−7·0	B8	815
Procyon	α CMi	07 37	05 21	0·35	2·7	F5	11
Achernar	α Eri	01 34	−57 45	0·48	−2·2	B5	127
Hadar	β Cen	14 00	−60 08	0·60	−5·0	B1	390
Altair	α Aql	19 48	08 44	0·77	2·3	A7	16
Betelgeuse	α Ori	05 53	07 24	0·8	−6·0	M2	650
Aldebaran	α Tau	04 33	16 25	0·85	−0·7	K5	69
Acrux	α Cru	12 24	−62 49	0·9	−3·5	B2	260
Spica	α Vir	13 23	−10 54	0·96	−3·4	B1	260
Antares	α Sco	16 26	−26 19	1·0	−4·7	M1	425
Pollux	β Gem	07 42	28 09	1·15	1·0	K0	36
Fomalhaut	α PsA	22 55	−29 53	1·16	1·9	A3	23
Deneb	α Cyg	20 40	45 06	1·25	−7·3	A2	1630
Mimosa	β Cru	12 45	−59 25	1·26	−4·7	B0	490
Regulus	α Leo	10 06	12 14	1·35	−0·6	B7	85
Adhara	ε CMa	06 57	−28 54	1·50	−5·0	B2	650
Castor	α Gem	07 31	32 00	1·58	0·8	A1	46
Shaula	λ Sco	17 30	−37 04	1·62	−3·4	B1	325
Bellatrix	γ Ori	05 23	06 18	1·63	−3·3	B2	303

BRIGHT VARIABLES

Star		RA h m	Dec ° '	Magnitude range	Period (days)	Type
α	Cas	00 38	56 16	2—2·5	—	IRR
γ	Cas	00 54	60 27	1·6—3·2	—	IRR
ζ	Phe	01 06	−55 31	3·6—4·1	1·7	EBA
ο	Cet	02 17	−03 12	1·7—10·1	332	LPM
ρ	Per	03 02	38 39	3·3—4·2	33—55	SR
β	Per	03 05	40 46	2·2—3·5	2·9	EBA
λ	Tau	03 58	12 21	3·3—4·2	4	EBA
ε	Aur	04 58	43 45	3·3—4·2	9900	EBA
α	Ori	05 53	07 24	0·2—1	~2070	SR
ζ	Gem	07 01	20 39	3·7—4·3	10·2	C
R	Car	09 31	−62 34	3·9—10	381	LPM
l	Car	09 44	−62 17	3·6—5	35·5	C
R	Hya	13 27	−23 01	4—10	386	LPM
α	Her	17 12	14 27	3—4	?	SR
β	Lyr	18 48	33 18	3·4—4·1	12·9	EBB
χ	Cyg	19 49	32 47	3·3—14	407	LPM
η	Aql	19 50	00 53	3·7—4·7	7·2	C
μ	Cep	21 42	58 33	3·6—5·1	—	IRR
δ	Cep	22 27	58 10	3·6—4·3	5·4	C
ρ	Cas	23 52	57 13	4·1—6·2	—	?

IRR = irregular variable.   EBA = eclipsing binary, Algol type.   LPM = long-period variable, Mira type.
SR = semi-regular variable.   C = Cepheid.   EBB = eclipsing binary, β Lyrae type.

INTERESTING NEBULAE AND GALAXIES

Object		RA h m	Dec ° '	Magnitude	Remarks
M31	And	00 40	41 00	4·8	Andromeda Neb – Sb Gal
M32	And	00 40	40 36	8·7	E2 Gal
M33	Tri	01 31	30 24	6·7	Sc Gal
M77	Cet	02 40	−00 14	8·9	Sb Gal
M1	Tau	05 32	31 59	8·4	Crab Neb
M42	Ori	05 33	−05 25	4·0	Orion Neb
NGC2070	Dor	05 39	−69 09	6	Looped Neb
NGC2237	Mon	06 30	04 52	7	Rosette Neb
M81	UMa	09 52	69 18	8	Sb Gal
M82	UMa	09 52	69 56	8·8	Irreg Gal
M96	Leo	10 44	12 05	9	Sa Gal
M97	UMa	11 12	55 17	12	Owl Neb
M49	Vir	12 27	08 16	8·6	E1 Gal
M87	Vir	12 28	12 40	9·2	Giant E0 Gal
M104	Vir	12 37	−11 21	8·7	Sombrero Gal (Sb)
M94	CVn	12 49	41 24	7·9	Sb Gal
M64	Com	12 54	21 57	6·6	Black-eye Gal (Sb)
M51	CVn	13 28	47 27	8	Whirlpool Gal (Sc)
M20	Sgr	17 59	−23 02	9	Trifid Neb
M8	Sgr	18 00	−24 23	6	Lagoon Neb
M17	Sgr	18 18	−16 12	7	Omega Neb
M57	Lyr	18 52	32 58	9	Ring Neb
M27	Vul	19 57	22 35	8	Dumb-bell Neb
NGC7000	Cyg	20 57	44 11	9	North American Neb
NGC7009	Aqr	21 01	−11 34	8	Saturn Neb

COLOURED DOUBLE STARS

Star	RA h m	Dec ° '	Magnitudes	Separation	Colours
β Tuc	00 29	−63 14	4·5, 4·5	27	B, W
55 Psc	00 37	21 10	5·6, 8·8	7	O, B
η Cas	00 46	57 33	3·6, 7·5	10	Y, P
χ UMi	01 49	89 02	2·0, 9·0	18	Y, B
γ And	02 01	42 06	2·3, 5·1	10	O, B
η Per	02 47	55 41	3·9, 8·6	28	Y, B
β Ori	05 12	−08 15	0·2, 7·0	9	B, B
χ Gem	07 31	32 00	2·0, 2·9	5	W, W
γ Leo	10 17	20 06	2·6, 3·8	4	Y, G
χ Cru	12 24	−62 49	1·6, 2·1	5	B, B
χ Cen	14 36	−60 38	0·0, 1·7	4	Y, R
χ Sco	16 26	−26 19	1·2, 6·5	3	R, G
χ Her	17 12	14 27	var, 5·4	5	R, G
ψ Dra	17 43	72 11	4·9, 6·1	30	Y, B
ε Lyr	18 43	39 37	4·7, 4·5	208	Y, B
β Cyg	19 29	27 52	3·2, 5·4	35	Y, G
ε Dra	19 48	70 08	4·0, 7·1	3	Y, B
χ Cap	20 15	−12 40	3·7, 4·5	376	Y, Y
β Cep	21 28	70 20	3·3, 8·0	14	G, B
δ Cep	22 27	58 10	var, 7·5	40	Y, B

B = blue   W = white   O = orange   Y = yellow   P = purple   R = red   G = green

Double Stars

Many stars which appear as single points of light to the naked eye resolve into two components when viewed through a telescope. Such a star is called a double star. Although the two components may appear to be close together, they need not necessarily be so. They may just happen to be in our line of sight and in reality be a great distance apart. Such line-of-sight doubles are termed 'optical pairs', or 'optical doubles'.

The double stars that do consist of components physically associated with one another are called binaries. Each component revolves around a common centre of gravity for the system. The heavens abound in binaries – in fact, nearly half the stars are binaries. The middle star in the handle of the Plough, Mizar, is a binary, easily visible in a low-powered telescope. With Alcor, Mizar also forms an optical and naked-eye double. Albireo in Cygnus, is another fine binary, which can just be separated in binoculars. It is one of many binary pairs which differ markedly in colour. Two of the other prominent stars in Cygnus are doubles – δ is a close binary, while γ is a wide optical double.

The ease with which the components of a double system can be separated depends on the resolving power of the telescope being used (see page 113). But the components of

η Cassiopeiae

φ Tauri

β Cygni

MIZAR – A MULTIPLE STAR SYSTEM

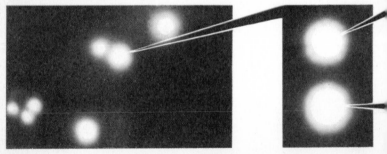

Mizar, the middle star in the handle of the Plough, forms a naked-eye optical pair with Alcor. When viewed through a telescope, however, Mizar resolves into twin components. Examination of the spectra of the components reveals that each is a spectroscopic binary.

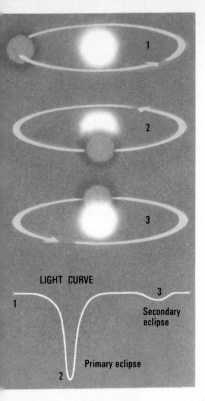

ECLIPSING BINARIES

Some binary star systems revolve in a plane that causes the components to eclipse each other periodically when viewed from the Earth. The overall brightness of the system decreases during eclipse. If one component is much brighter than the other, a dramatic change in brightness occurs during eclipse of the bright component.

The first star of this type to be recognised was Algol, in Perseus. It varies between about magnitudes 2 and 3 in a little under 3 days. Its characteristic light output is shown on the left. There are two drops in brightness – the main one at the primary eclipse of the bright component, the other at the secondary eclipse of the dimmer component.

Another type of eclipsing binary is β Lyrae. This has its components so close together that they are distorted by tidal forces into elliptical shapes and enveloped by gas. The light output of the system varies continuously. Most eclipsing binaries are of the Algol or β Lyrae types and are so described. Their periods of variability vary widely.

Eclipsing binaries form one class of variable stars. They differ from true variables, which vary in brightness because of processes going on inside them (see page 52).

LIGHT CURVE

Secondary eclipse

Primary eclipse

some binaries are too close to be separated by even the most powerful telescopes. They reveal their dual nature only in their spectrum, which changes in a regular manner. Such stars are called spectroscopic binaries. Castor, in Gemini, is a visual binary, whose twin components each prove to be spectroscopic binaries. And there is a third spectroscopic binary close by, making a six-star system in all.

There are many other examples of multiple-star systems like this, including Mizar. α Capricorni is also an interesting system. It is a naked-eye double. And each of its components is double – one an optical pair, the other a binary. The fainter component of the binary is itself a binary.

Variable Stars

While the majority of stars shine steadily century after century, some do not. Their brightness changes, often dramatically, over a period of a few days, months or years. The eclipsing binary (page 51) is one type of variable star, but its variation in brightness has an external cause. It is called an extrinsic variable.

Other variables vary in brightness because of internal processes – usually expansion and contraction – and are thus called intrinsic variables. The fluctuations in brightness may be regular or irregular and the degree of fluctuation large or small. Several different classes of variables can be recognized whose member stars behave in a similar fashion. They may be named after the star in which the characteristic variation was first observed, or after the way they vary (see below). A rather different class of variable stars includes those that suddenly explode – novae (new stars) and supernovae.

It is in the field of variable stars that the amateur astronomer comes into his own, particularly as far as the unpredictable irregular variables are concerned. Professional astronomers do not have the time to catalogue the vagaries of these celestial mavericks.

When observing variable stars, an estimate of their brightness must always be attempted. This is done using nearby stars, whose magnitudes are known, for comparison. Ideally, several comparison stars should be chosen – of different magnitudes, slightly brighter and slightly dimmer than the variable. An estimate of the variable's brightness is then obtained by glancing at the comparison stars and the variable in turn to see where it fits in. To eliminate error, due for example to colour differences, the same comparison stars should be chosen each time.

The Crab nebula in Taurus.

TYPES OF VARIABLE STARS

Cepheids are named after delta Cephei, a regular-as-clockwork variable whose magnitude varies between 3·5 and 4·3 in $5\frac{1}{3}$ days. 'Classical' Cepheids have periods of variation ranging from about 2–50 days. Short-period Cepheids, typified by RR Lyrae, have periods of $0·2–1\frac{1}{2}$ days; dwarf Cepheids have even shorter periods. The most interesting thing about Cepheids is that their period of variation is related directly to their absolute magnitude. So wherever a Cepheid is found, its distance can be calculated by comparing its observed visual magnitude with its inferred absolute magnitude.

Below: Light curve of a Cepheid.

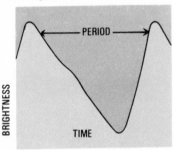

Mira Ceti variables provide a greater variation in brightness. They are long-period variables which often take a few hundred days to complete their cycle. Mira Ceti, for example, fluctuates from approximately mag 3 to 10 in about 331 days. Like the other members of this class it is a red giant.

Irregular and semi-regular variables The period of Mira Ceti stars is not as regular as the Cepheids, but does not vary by more than a few days. The periods of other variables can vary by months and even years. Betelgeuse in Orion is a semi-regular variable, changing between magnitudes 0·2 and 1 in about 6 years. Other variables are totally irregular, suddenly brightening or dimming unpredictably. A notable case are the R Coronae Borealis stars which shine steadily most of the time and then suddenly dim by 5–8 magnitudes.

Novae So-called new stars, novae are actually faint existing stars that suddenly explode and increase in brightness by at least 10,000 times. After a few nights they begin to fade, but take years to return to their original magnitude. On average, two or three are seen each year, but only a few are really bright. The brightest novae this century were in Perseus (1901, mag 0), Aquila (1918, mag 0·7), and Puppis (1942, mag 0·4).

Below: Gases from nova Persei, 1901

Recurrent Novae Some novae have been known to erupt explosively more than once and are called recurrent novae. Most notable perhaps is T Coronae Borealis, which is normally mag 10, but reached mag 2 in 1866 and mag 3 in 1946.

Supernovae have been seen to occur in our galaxy only three times in the past thousand years – in Taurus in 1054, in Cassiopeia in 1572, and in Ophiuchus in 1604. Chinese astronomers recorded the first, and its remnants are the Crab Nebula. In a supernova explosion, an increase of 20 magnitudes may occur. For a while the star may be as bright as a whole galaxy. A bright supernova was observed in the Large Magellanic Cloud in 1987. Pulsars are thought to be the stellar remains of supernova explosions (see page 119).

Star Clusters

Above: The M13 cluster.
Opposite: The Pleiades.
Below: The double cluster in Perseus.

In general, stars tend to be highly gregarious. Many exist in space with one or more close companions. Many also form part of a much wider stellar system, which we term a cluster. The rather loosely knit open clusters usually contain tens or hundreds of members which travel through space together. The most prominent open cluster is the famous Pleiades, in Taurus, which is clearly visible to the naked eye. Like most open clusters, it is made up of relatively young stars.

In contrast are the globular clusters that surround the centre of the Galaxy. They are great globes made up of hundreds of thousands of much older stars packed together. The brightest globular clusters in the heavens include ω Centauri and 47 Tucanae in the southern hemisphere, and M13 in Hercules in the northern hemisphere. All three are clearly visible to the naked eye although they are some tens of thousands of light-years away. Most globulars lie towards Sagittarius in the direction of the centre of the Galaxy. An odd feature of globulars is that they rotate around the galactic centre independently of the rest of the stars.

FAMOUS CLUSTERS

Double cluster in Perseus Also known as the Sword-Handle, a fine pair of clusters visible to the naked eye in Perseus between α Persei and δ Cassiopeia. They are designated h Persei and χ Persei (NGC869 and 884).

Hyades A scattered open cluster in Taurus, clearly visible to the naked eye around the red giant star Aldebaran. It is close enough (140 light-years) for its bodily motion to be detected.

Pleiades The finest and brightest cluster of all (M45), also in Taurus. Known as the Seven Sisters because keen-eyed people can pick out its seven brightest stars, it actually contains several hundred members. It is a glorious sight in binoculars.

Praesepe A much fainter but still visible open cluster in Cancer (M44), roughly midway between Pollux in Gemini and Regulus in Leo. It is nicknamed the Beehive.

Jewel Box Around the reddish star κ Crucis, a beautiful open cluster of stars of various colours that sparkle like jewels (NGC4755).

Wild Duck A dense fan-shaped cluster in Scutum (M11), just visible to the naked eye and superb in binoculars.

INTERESTING CLUSTERS

Object		RA h m	Dec ° '	Magnitude	Type	Object		RA h m	Dec ° '	Magnitude	Type
NGC104	Tuc	00 22	−72 22	5	Glob	M53	Com	13 10	18 26	7·6	Glob
NGC362	Tuc	01 01	−71 06	6	Glob	NGC5139	Cen	13 24	−47 03	3·7	Glob
M103	Cas	01 30	60 27	7·5	Open	M3	CVn	13 40	28 38	6·4	Glob
NGC869	Per	02 17	56 55	4·4	Open	M5	Ser	15 16	02 16	6·2	Glob
NGC884	Per	02 20	56 53	4·7	Open	NGC6025	TrA	15 59	−60 21	5	Open
M34	Per	02 39	42 34	5·5	Open	M4	Sco	16 21	−26 24	6·4	Glob
M45	Tau	03 44	24	1·6	Open	M13	Her	16 40	36 33	5·7	Glob
—	Tau	04 18	15	3	Open	M92	Her	17 16	43 12	6	Glob
M37	Aur	05 49	32 32	6·2	Open	M6	Sco	17 37	−32 11	5·3	Open
M35	Gem	06 06	24 21	5·3	Open	M7	Sco	17 51	−34 48	4	Open
M41	CMa	06 45	−20 41	4·6	Open	M22	Sgr	18 33	−23 58	6	Glob
M44	Cnc	08 37	20 00	3·7	Open	M11	Sct	18 48	−06 20	6·3	Open
NGC3766	Cen	11 34	−61 20	5	Open	M15	Peg	21 28	11 57	6	Glob
M68	Hya	12 37	−26 29	8·2	Glob	M39	Cyg	21 30	48 13	5·2	Open
NGC4755	Cru	12 51	−60 05	5	Open	M52	Cas	23 22	61 19	7·3	Open

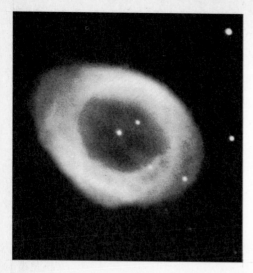

Nebulae

Left: The Ring nebula in Lyra.

Right: The Great nebula in Orion.

Bottom right: The Horsehead nebula, also in Orion.

Many of the star clusters are visible only as misty patches, and early astronomers can be forgiven for calling them nebulae, or clouds. But other misty patches in the heavens *are* clouds of glowing gas. The easiest to spot is the great nebula in Orion, visible to the naked eye below the 'belt' of Orion. A few other nebulae are just bright enough to be seen with the naked eye, including the Looped nebula in Doradus and the Lagoon nebula in Sagittarius. Several other nebulae can be viewed with binoculars or a low-power telescope, including the North American nebula in Cygnus; the Ring nebula in Lyra; the Trifid nebula and Omega nebula in Sagittarius; and the Dumb-bell nebula in Vulpecula.

The clouds that form a nebula consist of gas and dust. The gas is mainly hydrogen and the dust specks of graphite (carbon). Nebulae are concentrations of the interstellar matter that exists between the stars. Taken as a whole, interstellar matter can account for up to a fifth of the total mass of a galaxy.

Most of the prominent nebulae are emission nebulae. They absorb energy from stars embedded within them and emit light of characteristic wavelength. Other nebulae merely reflect light from nearby stars and are thus not so striking. A third type of nebula presents a planet-like disc at first glance and is called a planetary. The 'disc' is actually a spherical shell of expanding gas which is the result of an earlier explosion of a central star. The Dumb-bell and Ring nebulae are fine examples.

A fourth type of nebula does not shine at all but reveals its presence by obscuring the light of stars beyond it. Such dark nebulae cause the apparent rifts in the Milky Way – for example in Cygnus. The 'hole' in the Milky Way near the Southern Cross is a dark nebula, known as the Coal Sack. The aptly named Horsehead is a dark nebula in Orion.

INTERSTELLAR MOLECULES
In recent years, radio astronomers have detected the presence of a variety of molecules in interstellar space. These molecules signal their presence by emitting characteristic radiation at wavelengths which radio telescopes can pick up (see page 118). Among the compounds found are water, alcohol, carbon sulphide, silicon oxide, formaldehyde and methylamine. The presence of organic molecules in space came as a shock. It suggests that life could be more abundant in the universe than was once thought.

The Milky Way

If you gaze at the sky on a really dark night, you can see a hazy silvery band arching overhead. We call it the Milky Way. If you look at it in binoculars or a telescope, it resolves into millions of stars. This star band represents a cross-section of the galaxy or star system, to which all the stars in the sky belong. The Milky Way takes the form of a tapering disc with a central bulge, and would look from a distance rather like two fried eggs placed back to back.

The centre of the Galaxy lies in the direction of Sagittarius and it is in this and the neighbouring constellation Scorpio that the Milky Way is brightest. In these constellations, the stars are packed so densely that they give the appearance of a continuous bright cloud. In the northern hemisphere, the Milky Way is brightest in Cygnus and Aquila. It is very uneven in width and in places is split and holed. Such rifts are caused by the presence of intervening clouds (nebulae) of interstellar matter that blot out light from beyond.

The 100,000 million stars that make up the Galaxy are not evenly distributed, but congregate in curving arms that spiral outwards from the galactic centre. There are many such spiral galaxies in the universe. The galactic nebulae and other interstellar matter are concentrated in the

Left: A brilliant star cloud in Sagittarius. The streak marked the path of a satellite.

Right: The region of the Milky Way near Crux, showing the Coal Sack.

plane of the starry disc. The globular clusters, however, are not. They are distributed in a great enveloping sphere around the disc, particularly around the central bulge.

Globular clusters pursue an independent existence, orbiting separately around the galactic centre. The other stars rotate in the plane of the disc, which thus takes the form of a spinning Catherine Wheel. They travel faster the nearer they are to the galactic centre. The Sun, which lies towards the edge of the disc, takes 225 million years to circle the Galaxy, a period known as a cosmic year.

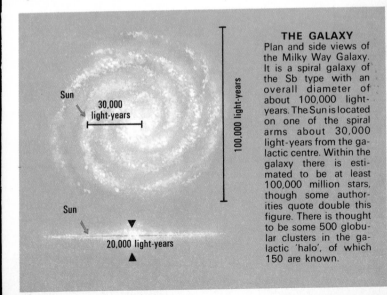

Sun

30,000 light-years

100,000 light-years

Sun

20,000 light-years

THE GALAXY
Plan and side views of the Milky Way Galaxy. It is a spiral galaxy of the Sb type with an overall diameter of about 100,000 light-years. The Sun is located on one of the spiral arms about 30,000 light-years from the ga-lactic centre. Within the galaxy there is esti-mated to be at least 100,000 million stars, though some author-ities quote double this figure. There is thought to be some 500 globu-lar clusters in the ga-lactic 'halo', of which 150 are known.

M31, the Andromeda nebula.

Outer Galaxies

Large Magellanic Cloud.

Just north of β Andromedae, close to the Square of Pegasus, is a large misty patch which has the appearance of a nebula. And it is in fact known as the Andromeda Nebula (M31). But powerful telescopes show it to be another star system beyond our Galaxy. It is a so-called extragalactic nebula, or outer galaxy. It is one of the few such galaxies that are visible to the naked eye. Two other notable examples are the Large and Small Magellanic Clouds, which lie close to the southern celestial pole.

Low-powered telescopes can reveal a host of other external galaxies – eg the Whirlpool galaxy in Canes Venatici; the Sombrero galaxy in Virgo; the Black-eye galaxy in Coma Berenices. More powerful telescopes can reveal the spiral nature of the closer galaxies and even resolve them into stars. They also reveal that regions of the heavens even contain clusters of galaxies.

Edwin Hubble, who did great pioneering work on galaxies in the 1920s, worked out the scheme of galactic classification which is still followed. It is based on the shapes of the galaxies. The three main classes are outlined below – ellipticals (E), spirals (S) and barred spirals (Sb). Our own Galaxy and Andromeda are examples of the Sb type, with reasonably well-defined spiral arms. The Large and Small Magellanic Clouds, however, are quite different. They have no definite structure and are termed irregular.

These latter galaxies are our closest galactic neighbours, being only some 170,000 and 205,000 light-years away. This compares with over 2,200,000 light-years for Andromeda. The Magellanic Clouds are very much smaller than our own Galaxy, while the Andromeda galaxy is about the same size. Most galaxies are 'dwarfs', so small and dim that only the closest ones can be detected.

Even though the Andromeda galaxy is so far away, it forms part of the group of galaxies that includes our own and the Magellanic Clouds. This Local Group contains

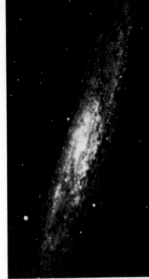

Sc galaxy in Sculptor.

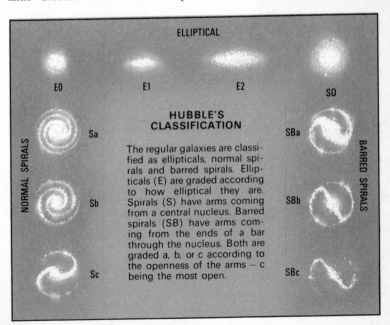

ELLIPTICAL

E0   E1   E2   S0

HUBBLE'S CLASSIFICATION

NORMAL SPIRALS

Sa   Sb   Sc

BARRED SPIRALS

SBa   SBb   SBc

The regular galaxies are classified as ellipticals, normal spirals and barred spirals. Ellipticals (E) are graded according to how elliptical they are. Spirals (S) have arms coming from a central nucleus. Barred spirals (SB) have arms coming from the ends of a bar through the nucleus. Both are graded a, b, or c according to the openness of the arms – c being the most open.

some 20 galaxies within a radius of about $2\frac{1}{2}$ million light-years. Many other galaxies belong to groups which, in exceptional cases, contain hundreds of members. The largest cluster of galaxies known occurs in Virgo and contains up to 3000 members. The Coma Berenices–Virgo region is particularly rich in galaxies, as can readily be observed even in a low-power telescope.

As might be expected, estimating distances to the remote galaxies is usually difficult. Where stars can be resolved and Cepheid-type stars found, the distance can be found by the period-luminosity relationship (page 53). Other estimates rely on assumptions about the average brightness of bright stars if they can be resolved, or the overall brightness of the galaxy if they cannot. But the most valuable method of estimating galactic distances is by the pronounced red shift in the spectrum of their light (see below). The red shift indicates that all the galaxies, apart from the Local Group, are fast receding from us in all directions. This suggests that the universe is expanding, as if from some primordial explosion, or 'big bang'.

Left: A cluster of galaxies in Hercules.
Bottom left: M51, the Whirlpool galaxy.

RED SHIFT
When the light from a star or a galaxy is passed through a spectroscope, it is split into a coloured spectrum marked by thin black lines, which are characteristic of certain elements in the star's atmosphere. When the star or galaxy is receding from us, its light appears to be of longer wavelength than if it were stationary (the Doppler effect). This causes the spectral lines to shift towards the red end of the spectrum. The extent of this red shift is a measure of the speed of recession. When the spectrum of light from galaxies a known distance away is examined, it is found that the red shift is directly proportional to the distance of the galaxy. A galaxy three times as far away as another travels three times as fast. Assuming this relationship holds for all galaxies at all distances, then the distance to remote galaxies can be determined by measuring the extent of the red shift.

THE BIG BANG

The observed expansion of the universe forms the starting point for theories of how the universe came into being and subsequently evolved. Most cosmogonists – astronomers who study the origin and development of the universe – now favour an evolutionary,

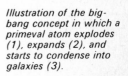

Illustration of the big-bang concept in which a primeval atom explodes (1), expands (2), and starts to condense into galaxies (3).

or 'big-bang' theory, according to which all the matter in the universe was once concentrated into a 'primeval atom' which suffered a catastrophic explosion some time in the past. The explosion, or fireball, created the universe as matter was ejected in an ever-expanding shell. As the expansion proceeded the matter cooled down and pockets of it began to condense into galaxies, receding all the while. Radio astronomers have found some evidence to support a big bang in the background radiation that permeates the whole of interstellar space.

Projecting backwards from the present state of expansion, we can derive an approximate date for the 'big bang'. It works out at something like 10–15,000 million years ago, or two to three times the age of the solar system. The exact age remains uncertain, however, and it could be as high as 20,000 million years. If the red

shift of quasars is being correctly interpreted (page 119), objects have already been found that lie at least 10,000 million light-years away and so must have been in existence for more than 16,000 million years.

Some astronomers have extended the big-bang concept and postulate an oscillating universe. The expansion of the universe will one day be arrested, they say, and then contraction will set in, resulting ultimately in the creation of another primeval atom. This will again explode, and a new expansion phase will begin. This kind of oscillation will continue indefinitely, in something like a 80,000 million year cycle. But observations suggest that there is not enough matter in the existing universe to be able to slow down the galaxies by gravitation, though this could be hidden in black holes.

An alternative explanation to the 'big bang' is the steady-state theory, according to which the universe has always existed and will continue for ever. Matter is being created all the time so that the average density of the universe remains the same as it expands.

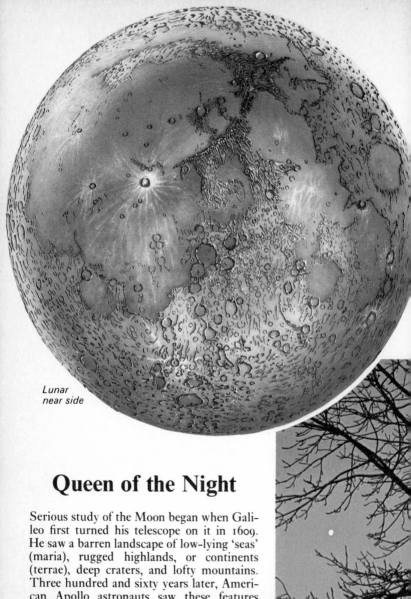

Lunar
near side

Queen of the Night

Serious study of the Moon began when Galileo first turned his telescope on it in 1609.
He saw a barren landscape of low-lying 'seas'
(maria), rugged highlands, or continents
(terrae), deep craters, and lofty mountains.
Three hundred and sixty years later, American Apollo astronauts saw these features
close-to as they explored the dusty lunar surface on foot. The Apollo lunar-landing project reaped a rich harvest in scientific knowledge, though opinions are sharply divided on

whether it was worth the 25,000 million dollars lavished on it.

The Moon, Earth's nearest neighbour in space and its only satellite, lies at an average distance of about 384,000 km (239,000 mi). It has about one quarter the diameter of the Earth, and at its surface, gravity is only one-sixth that of the Earth. Nevertheless, the Moon is still massive enough to exert an appreciable gravitational attraction on the Earth. This manifests itself in the tides, the rhythmic rise and fall of the ocean waters twice a day.

Because the Moon is so small and its gravity so weak, it cannot retain any atmosphere, so on the Moon there can be no sound or weather. Temperatures vary greatly. In the two-week lunar 'day', surface temperatures soar to over 100°C, while in the two-week lunar 'night' they may plummet to −150°C.

The Moon has a captured rotation, which means that it always presents the same face to us (see page 68). We see more or less of this

Above: An ancient plani-sphere for computing the Moon's phases.

Below: A gibbous Moon in the early morning sky.

Lunar far side

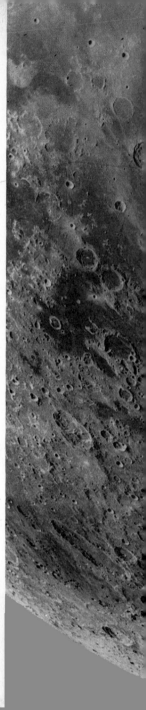

face illuminated during the month, depending on the position of the Moon in relation to the Sun, because the Moon shines by reflected sunlight. The boundary between the dark and the illuminated surface is known as the terminator. As the Moon goes through its changing aspects, or phases, the terminator scans across the surface.

Observation of the Moon is rewarding even with the naked eye, which can clearly distinguish the dark mare regions and the lighter-coloured highlands. With binoculars, a wealth of detail becomes visible – walled craters, sinuous rilles, mountain chains and crater rays. Increasing magnification in telescopes provides the viewer with breathtaking lunar landscapes. They are all the more fascinating because they change night by night as the angle of illumination changes.

The greatest detail can be seen near the terminator. Then, the mountain ranges show up in profile and cast shadows from which their height can be estimated. Craters too are most prominent near the terminator when their floors are shadow-filled. Under higher angles of illumination, they become indistinct and may even disappear. So full moon is not a good time to view the lunar surface.

From the astronomical point of view, the Moon is something of an oddity. It is really too big to be an ordinary satellite. The satellites of the other planets are mostly tens of thousands of times less massive than their planet. Yet the Moon is only 81 times less massive. It was once thought that the Moon was torn from the Earth, but this seems highly unlikely. Moon rocks differ considerably from terrestrial rocks, being much richer in such metals as chromium, titanium and zirconium and radioactive metals such as uranium and thorium. Many astronomers think that the Moon was once another planet, and that the Earth–Moon should be considered a double planetary system.

Telescopic view of the Moon showing Mare Nubium (top) and the highlands south of it.

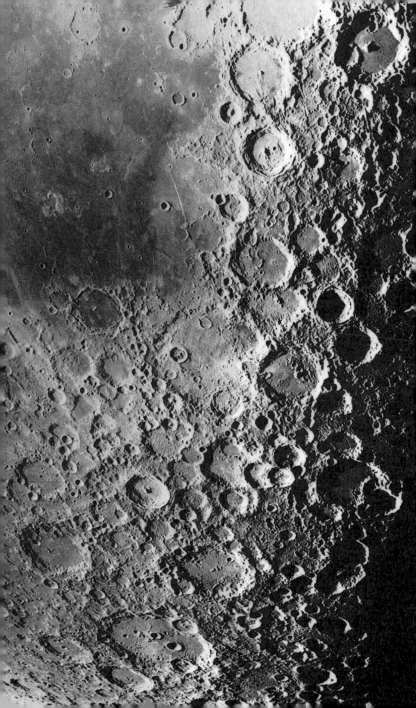

MOTIONS OF THE MOON

The Moon has two movements in space: (1) it spins on its axis, and (2) it revolves around the Earth. It takes $27\frac{1}{3}$ days to spin once on its axis and the same period (sidereal month) to revolve once around the Earth relative to the stars. Because the two periods are the same, the Moon always presents the same face to us.

As the Moon travels in its orbit around the Earth, we see different parts of it illuminated because of its changing position relative to the Sun. These changing aspects of the Moon are called its phases (see below). When the Moon lies in the direction of the Sun, it presents a dark face towards us (new moon). Gradually a slim crescent appears, which grows to a half moon in about a week (first quarter). A week later, the whole face is lit up (full moon). Then the lit portion gradually recedes to a half moon (last quarter) until it finally disappears at the next new moon.

The Moon goes through its phases in $29\frac{1}{2}$ days. This is known as the synodic month. It is the Moon's period of revolution around the Earth relative to the Sun. It is longer than the sidereal month, because the Earth itself is moving around the Sun and it takes the Moon an extra two days to return to the same position relative to the Sun.

The Moon's orbit around the Earth does not lie in quite the same plane as the Earth's orbit around the Sun. If it did, solar eclipses (page 111) would occur regularly at each new moon. The axis on which the Moon rotates is not quite perpendicular to its orbital plane. This means that, as it travels in its orbit, the Moon appears to 'nod' slightly, enabling us to see a little more north and south than we otherwise could. This 'nodding' motion is called libration in latitude.

There is also a libration in longitude, which enables us to see a little around the

Crescent, 4 days   *First quarter, 7 days*

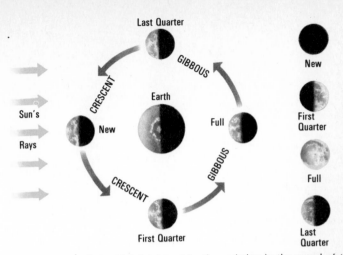

eastern and western limbs. This is caused by the variation in the speed of the Moon in its elliptical orbit — it travels fastest when it is nearest (at perigee) and slowest when it is farthest (at apogee). Thanks to these librations, we can see a total of 59% of the lunar surface during the month.

Full moon, 14 days   *Last quarter, 21 days*

LUNAR FEATURES

Craters The most common lunar features, most of which resulted from meteorite impact. They vary in size from a few metres up to more than 250 km across. The larger ones, such as Tycho and Copernicus, have high terraced walls, a deeply sunken floor and a central mountain group. Large craters with low walls and shallower floors are often known as walled, or ring plains. Chain craters are lines of small craters resembling a string of beads. They are often linked by rilles.

Depressions Small circular crater-like features but without raised rims, found only in the maria. Often called dimple craters.

Domes Raised circular bulges mainly restricted to the maria, which may be several kilometres in diameter but seldom more than 100 metres in height. They tend to cluster in groups and many are capped with craterlets. They resemble terrestrial laccoliths, or lava blisters.

Faults Dislocations in the surface where one segment of the lunar crust has slipped relative to another. The best-known fault is the Straight Wall in Mare Nubium.

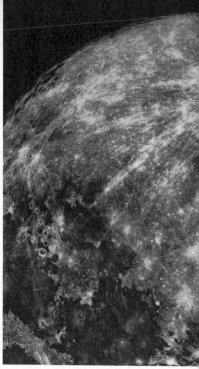

Above: Prominent rays emanate from the crater Tycho at full moon.
Left: Alpine Valley.
Right: Hyginus Rille in Sinus Medii.

MOON DATA	
Equatorial diameter:	3476 km, 2160 mi
Volume:	1/49 Earth's volume
Mean density:	3·3 (water = 1)
Mass:	1/81 Earth's mass
Surface gravity:	1/6 Earth's gravity
Perigee distance:	356,400 km, 221,460 mi
Apogee distance:	406,700 km, 252,710 mi
Mean distance:	384,400 km, 238,860 mi
Spins on axis in:	$27\frac{1}{3}$ days
Orbits Earth in	$27\frac{1}{3}$ days
Goes through its phases in:	$29\frac{1}{2}$ days
Apparent magnitude:	−12·7
Escape velocity:	2·4 km/sec, 1·5 mi/sec

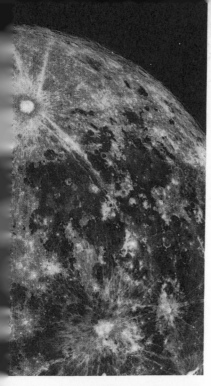

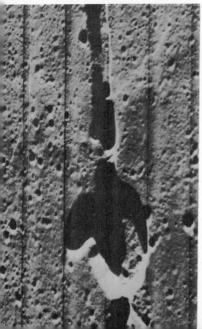

Maria The lunar 'seas' — the dark regions of the Moon we see from Earth. They are smooth, low-lying regions marked by relatively few large craters, of circular (e.g. Mare Crisium) or irregular (e.g. Mare Frigoris) shape. They are of more recent origin than the lunar highlands (terrae) and were probably formed by the re-melting of the original crust. No major maria occur on the Moon's far side. The typical mare rock, lunabase, resembles the terrestrial volcanic rock, basalt.

Mascons Regions of the surface of unusually high gravity that indicate the presence of concentrations of high-density material. They are found primarily in the maria.

Mountains The greater part of the Moon's surface is mountainous. Most spectacular are the ranges bordering the maria, particularly Mare Imbrium. This is ringed by the lofty Caucasus, Apennine and Carpathian ranges, and the lunar Alps. Peaks in the Caucasus rise to 6000 metres (20,000 ft). But the highest lunar peaks, in the Leibnitz Mountains near the south pole, soar to 8000 metres (26,000 ft). Many large craters have a central mountain range, while on the maria isolated peaks can occur.

Rays Long white streaks that radiate from many of the large craters, particularly Copernicus, Kepler and Tycho. They are thought to be made up of glassy material ejected when the craters were formed.

Rilles Long trenches, probably of volcanic origin, which occur commonly on the maria. Normal rilles are relatively straight, while sinuous rilles meander like a river course. Typically, they are less than 5 km (3 mi) wide and 700 metres (2300 ft) deep, but can extend for 200 km (120 mi) or more. Most prominent is Hyginus Rille in Sinus Medii.

Terrae The light-coloured highland regions, thought to be part of the Moon's original crust. Its typical rock is lunarite, a cemented mixture of rock chips resembling terrestrial breccia.

TLPs Short for transient lunar phenomena. Ruddy glows and gaseous emissions that have been observed in the craters Aristarchus, Alphonsus, Plato and elsewhere. They provide evidence that the Moon is not wholly dead.

71

The Apollo Assaults

Lunarnauts at work: from Apollo 11 (below), 16 (left) and 17 (above).

The twelve Apollo astronauts who landed on the Moon between 1969 and 1972 roamed the surface for a total of 166 hours and brought back with them 385 kg (850 lb) of lunar rocks and soil. Not only did they conduct experiments while they were there, but they also set up automatic scientific stations which carried on functioning after they left. They also took some 30,000 photographs and collected 20,000 reels of taped instrument readings.

The first priorities of the Apollo astronauts were to collect specimens of rock and soil and bore into the surface to take core samples. The layers in the cores reflect the state of the lunar environment over periods of millions of years.

Setting up the automatic scientific stations was the next major priority. Known as ALSEP (Apollo lunar surface experiments package), these stations are made up of a variety of sensing instruments. They continue to send back data even now, though NASA is no longer collecting it. The instruments are connected to a central station which provides their power and transmits the data they collect back to Earth. The power derives from a thermoelectric nuclear generator known as SNAP-19, which has the radio-

active isotope plutonium-238 as its heat source.

The sensing instruments, which vary from station to station, include:

Laser reflector, to bounce laser beams back to Earth. By this means, scientists have estimated the Earth–Moon distance to within 15 cm (6 in).

Seismometer, to register seismic activity, or 'moonquakes', triggered off by the impact of meteorites or, initially, redundant Apollo hardware. Studies of the seismic waves reveal much about the Moon's make-up.

Magnetometer, to register magnetic fields. Local magnetic fields proved to be surprisingly strong and in different directions, which suggests that the Moon may once have had a strong magnetic field. It might, therefore, have had a molten iron core, like the Earth has now.

Ion and particle detectors, to detect the presence of charged and neutral particles near the surface. Such particles could come from the Sun as part of the solar wind or originate from cracks in the Moon's crust.

Heat-flow experiment, to determine the heat flow from the lunar interior. This has proved to be surprisingly high, suggesting that the Moon could have a small molten core. But it is more likely that it derives from a high concentration of radioactive elements in the lunar crust. The Moon's crust is in general somewhat more radioactive than the Earth's, particularly in certain areas, such as Copernicus.

THE APOLLO LANDINGS

No	Date	Landing site
11	Jul 1969	In south-west of Mare Tranquillitatis
12	Nov 1969	East of Landsberg crater, on lunar equator, in Oceanus Procellarum
13	Apr 1970	Mission aborted
14	Feb 1971	Fra Mauro crater, between Mare Nubium and Oceanus Procellarum
15	Jul 1971	Hadley Rille, in foothills of Apennines, on edge of Mare Imbrium
16	Apr 1972	Cayley Plains, in lunar highlands near Descartes crater
17	Dec 1972	On eastern edge of Mare Serenitatis, between Taurus Mountains and Littrow crater

Lunar Charts

Details of the lunar surface are described here and on the following pages, quadrant by quadrant. The illustrations show the surface as an observer would see it through a telescope, i.e. the lunar disc is inverted, with south at the top and north at the bottom. In accordance with a decision of the International Astronomical Union, lunar east is shown to the left and lunar west to the right. Many lunar maps show east and west the other way round, so care must be exercised when interpreting directions on a lunar chart.

Lunar Chart 1
South-East Quadrant

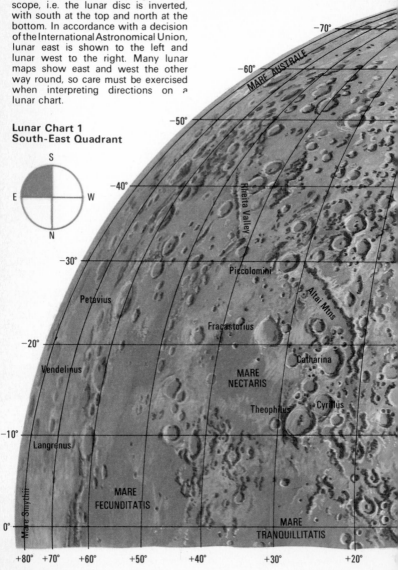

MARIA

Mare Fecunditatis (Sea of Fertility) is a relatively small, irregular shaped mare stretching for some 1000 km (600 mi) across the lunar equator. To the south-west is *Mare Nectaris* (Sea of Nectar). Almost circular and some 500 km (300 mi) across, this mare, like Fecunditatis, contains few prominent craters. When viewed with the naked eye and with binoculars, these two maria tend to merge with the huge *Mare Tranquillitatis* (see page 77).

Mare Australe (Southern Sea) is right on the south-east limb and is best seen just before or just after full moon. *Mare Smythii* (Smyth's Sea) similarly is right on the limb, straddling the equator. It is perhaps best seen when the Moon is only a few days old, when hills can be observed.

CRATERS

Langrenus (140 km, 85 mi dia) is one of three large walled craters along the eastern edge of Mare Fecunditatis. Its central mountain group becomes readily visible when the Moon is a few days old. So does that of *Petavius* (over 160 km, 100 mi), whose prominently terraced walls collapse in ruins in the north. The crater in between Langrenus and Petavius, *Vendelinus*, though of similar size, has a flat floor.

Due west of Petavius is another large unmistakable crater, *Fracastorius*, which forms a kind of bay of Mare Nectaris. One of Tycho's rays falls on the crater walls. Proceeding clockwise round this mare, we reach another ring of large prominent craters *Catharina*, *Cyrillus* and *Theophilus*, all about 100 km (60 mi) across. Theophilus is perhaps the most prominent, with a high central mountain range.

Due west of Theophilus is *Albategnius* with a small crater (*Klein*) in the eastern wall. It is smaller than the 160-km (100-mi) diameter *Hipparchus* immediately north of it. These craters are best seen at the terminator when the Moon is about 7 days old. Also prominent at this time are the almost equally large *Walter* and the twin circular 80-km (50-mi) *Aliacensis* and *Werner*. Farther south on the terminator at 7 days is the large *Stöfler*, ruined by the small *Faraday*. Faraday almost overlaps with the large *Maurolycus*, which has interesting terraces and off-centre mountain peaks. To the east of Maurolycus is the distinctive ruined *Janssen*, nearly 200 km (125 mi) across. Its walls enclose 90-km (55-mi) *Fabricius*, which adjoins the similar-size Metius.

Aliacensis is one of several craters in this quadrant that have high walls. They rise some 3600 m (12,000 ft) in the west and more than 5000 m (16,500 ft) in the east. *Piccolomini*, quite a distance to the east, has high terraced walls rising to some 4500 m (15,000 ft).

OTHER FEATURES

The *Altai Mountains* run north-west from Piccolomini some 500 km (300 mi) and reach a height of 4000 m (13,000 ft). Near the south-east limb is the 160-km (100-mi) long *Rheita Valley*, which skirts the deep 60-km (40-mi) crater *Rheita*.

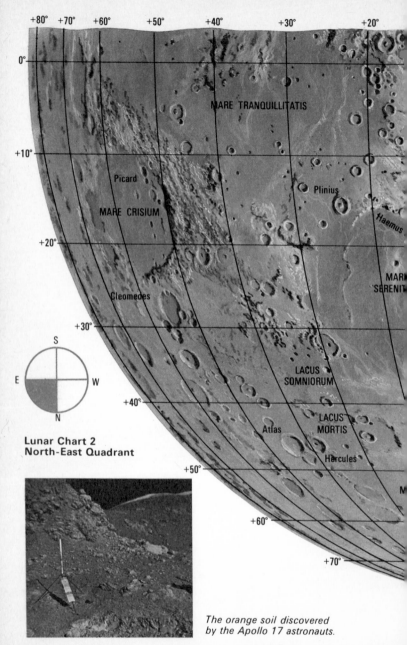

+80° +70° +60° +50° +40° +30° +20°

0°

MARE TRANQUILLITATIS

+10°

Picard

Plinius

MARE CRISIUM

Haemus

+20°

MARE
SERENIT

Cleomedes

+30°

S

E   W

LACUS
SOMNIORUM

N

+40°

Lunar Chart 2
North-East Quadrant

Atlas

LACUS
MORTIS

Hercules

+50°

M

+60°

+70°

*The orange soil discovered
by the Apollo 17 astronauts.*

76

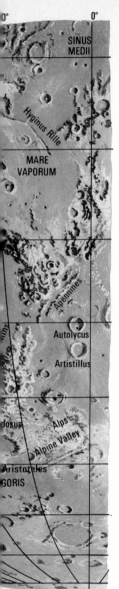

On the left image, the following labels are visible:

0°   0°

SINUS MEDII

Hyginus Rille

MARE VAPORUM

Apennines

Autolycus

Artistillus

Alps

Alpine Valley

Aristoteles

GORIS

MARIA

Three prominent maria dominate this quadrant. The two largest — *Mare Tranquillitatis* (Sea of Tranquillity) and *Mare Serenitatis* (Sea of Serenity) — are much the same size. They merge into one another in a region of low hills and small craters, the most prominent of which is *Plinius* (about 50 km, 30 mi dia). Mare Tranquillitatis was the location of the first Apollo Moon landing in 1969, which took place just south of the lunar equator at a longitude of about 25° East.

Mare Serenitatis has a more pronounced circular shape than Tranquillitatis, and has a diameter of about 600 km (400 mi). Its southern boundary is distinctly marked by the bordering *Haemus* and *Caucasus Mountains*. A faint crater ray running north-south bisects it.

To the east of Tranquillitatis lies the other major mare, *Crisium* (Sea of Crises). It, too, is distinctly circular, being about 500 km (300 mi) across. It contains only one prominent crater, the tiny *Picard* (about 30 km, 20 mi dia). Mare Crisium appears closer to the eastern limb at some times than at others, thus providing a vivid illustration of the Moon's libration (see page 69).

In the north Mare Serenitatis is linked via *Lacus Somniorum* (Lake of Sleep) and *Lacus Mortis* (Lake of Death) to the elongated irregular *Mare Frigoris* (Sea of Cold), which stretches west and south, eventually into *Oceanus Procellarum* (Ocean of Storms, see page 79).

The other mare in the quadrant, *Mare Vaporum* (Sea of Vapours) lies on the edge of the quadrant, south-west of Mare Serenitatis. It is quite small, but contains two of the most prominent lunar rilles, *Hyginus Rille* and *Ariadaeus Rille*. Right in the centre of the Moon at latitude 0°, longitude 0°, is the tiny mare-like *Sinus Medii*.

CRATERS

The quadrant has many fewer craters than the previous one, but some are quite interesting. Easily traceable when the Moon is a few days old is a ring of craters arcing north-west from Mare Crisium, of which the first *Cleomedes* is the largest (130 km, 80 mi dia). Adjacent to Lacus Mortis are the twin *Atlas* and *Hercules*, of which the former is somewhat larger at 90 km (55 mi) diameter.

West of these near-twins is the squarish *Aristoteles*, which borders Mare Frigoris. South of this is the smaller *Eudoxus*, which has a fine central peak and crater walls rising steeply to over 4300 metres (14,000 ft). Two smaller craters, *Aristillus* and *Autolycus* in *Palus Putredinis*, on the edge of Mare Imbrium (see page 81) form a prominent trio with Archimedes.

OTHER FEATURES

The *Caucasus Mountains* form a high boundary between Mare Serenitatis and Mare Imbrium. They rise in places to some 6000 metres (20,000 ft). Following the Caucasus mountains north-west around Mare Imbrium are the lunar *Alps*. These rise to a maximum 3600 metres (12,000 ft) near the 130-km (80-mi) long *Alpine Valley*. Curving south-west around this mare are the Apennines.

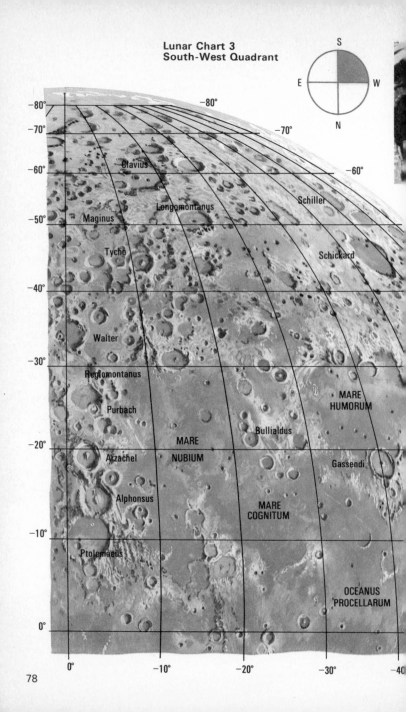

Lunar Chart 3
South-West Quadrant

S
E — W
N

-80°   -80°
-70°   -70°
            Clavius
-60°   -60°
                                Schiller
            Longomontanus
-50°   Maginus
                                Schickard
       Tycho

-40°

       Walter

-30°
    Regiomontanus
                                    MARE
                                    HUMORUM
       Purbach
                        Bullialdus
-20°
    Arzachel   MARE   Gassendi
               NUBIUM
    Alphonsus
                MARE
                COGNITUM
-10°
    Ptolemaeus

                                OCEANUS
                                PROCELLARUM
0°

0°   -10°   -20°   -30°   -40°

Microscopic cross-section of Apollo 11 Moon rock.

MARIA

The greater part of the Moon's western hemisphere consists of low-lying maria. In the south in this quadrant are the ill-defined *Mare Nubium* (Sea of Clouds) and the more circular *Mare Humorum* (Sea of Moisture).

Mare Nubium merges in the north-west with *Mare Cognitum* (Sea of Knowledge), usually considered a bay of the vast, sprawling *Oceanus Procellarum* (Ocean of Storms). At its eastern boundary is the prominent crater chain including *Ptolemaeus*. Mare Nubium's most interesting feature is the *Straight Wall* in the south-east, 100-km (60-mi) long and 240 metres (800 ft) high.

The larger part of the mare region in this quadrant, however, is occupied by Oceanus Procellarum, which extends far into the north-western quadrant. In all, it covers an area of some 5 million square km (2 million square miles), or roughly the area of the Mediterranean. Beyond the highland region round about latitude 20° south and right on the western limb is *Mare Orientale* (Eastern Sea). This circular mare can often be glimpsed just before the full moon. It is surrounded by the concentric *Cordillera* (outer) and *Rook Mountains*.

CRATERS

By no means the largest, but by far the most spectacular of the craters in this quadrant is *Tycho*, spectacular because of the shining rays that issue from it. They are best seen at full moon, when they radiate over the whole southern hemisphere and beyond. This 90-km (55-mi) dia crater has steep terraced walls some 4400 metres (14,500 ft) high.

Due south of Tycho is the Moon's largest crater *Clavius*, of over 230 km (140 mi) dia. Its walls and floor are heavily cratered. Tycho and Clavius make an easily recognizable 'cross' with near twins *Maginus* and *Longomontanus*. Longomontanus is slightly smaller than the 160-km (100-mi) dia Maginus, but has higher walls. Due west of Tycho is the very large *Schickard*, whose diameter is only about 16 km (10 mi) less than that of Clavius.

On the terminator at 7–8 days is the spectacular chain of large craters beginning, going north to south, with the 145-km (90-mi) dia *Ptolemaeus*. Then come *Alphonsus, Arzachel, Purbach,* and *Regiomontanus,* which nearly connects with *Walter* in the adjacent quadrant. These craters have diameters of about 110 km (70 mi), 95 km (60 mi), 120 km (75 mi) and 105 km (65 mi), respectively.

Among other craters of interest are the peculiarly elongated *Schiller* south-east of Schickard; the small (65 km, 40 mi) but deep and prominent *Bullialdus* on the edge of the Mare Nubium; the beautiful 90-km (55-mi) dia *Gassendi* on the edge of Mare Humorum; and the large pair *Grimaldi* (190 km, 120 mi) and *Riccioli* (160 km, 100 mi) near the western limb close to the lunar equator.

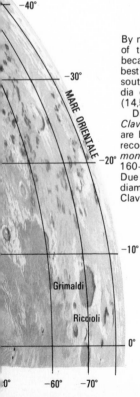

−40°

−30°

MARE ORIENTALE

−20°

−10°

Grimaldi

Riccioli

0°

0°   −60°   −70°

79

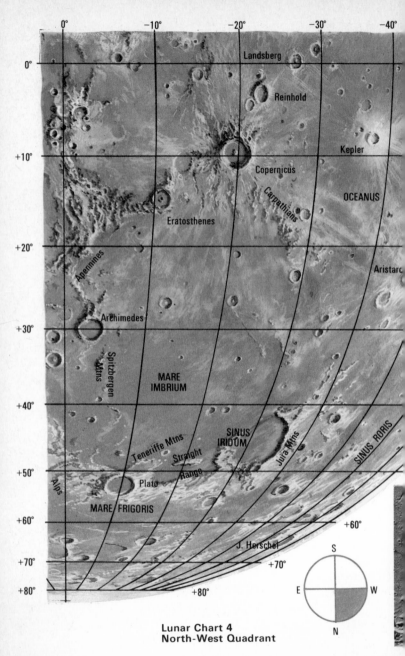

Lunar Chart 4
North-West Quadrant

80

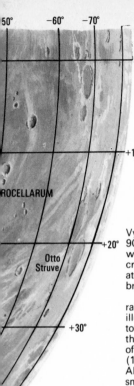

50°   −60°   −70°

0°

+10°

ROCELLARUM

+20°

Otto
Struve

+30°

+40°

*Typically flat and
lightly cratered
mare terrain.*

MARIA

Two massive maria occupy virtually the whole of this quadrant. There is the sprawling *Oceanus Procellarum* (Ocean of Storms), which extends from about 20° south in the previous quadrant into *Sinus Roris* at about 50° north, where it connects with the narrow *Mare Frigoris*.

Adjoining Oceanus Procellarum is the largest of the circular maria, *Mare Imbrium* (Sea of Showers), with a surface area of some 900,000 sq km (235,000 sq mi). It is ringed, except at its western edge, by steep mountains — the *Apennines* and *Carpathians* in the south, and the *Caucasus, Alps* and *Jura Mountains* in the north. The most prominent bay of this fine mare is *Sinus Iridum*, which is clearly marked by the Jura Mountains.

CRATERS

Vying with Tycho as the finest lunar crater is the splendid 90-km (56-mi) dia *Copernicus*, which has classic terraced walls that rise some 3900 metres (13,000 ft) from the crater floor. At full moon, sparkling white crater rays radiate from it, and the surrounding highland region is brilliantly lit.

To the west of Copernicus and also the source of crater rays is *Kepler* (35 km, 22 mi dia), which is also brilliantly illuminated at full moon. So is the similar-sized *Aristarchus* to the north-west, which is one of the brightest spots on the Moon. At the same latitude, close to the limb, is one of the quadrant's largest craters, the elongated 160-km (100-mi) dia *Otto Struve*, which is not at all prominent. Also close to the limb but much farther north is the slightly smaller *J. Herschel*. South-east of it is the prominent dark-floored *Plato* (100 km, 60 mi) on the edge of the Alps. The slightly smaller *Archimedes* farther south forms a conspicuous triangle with Autolycus and Aristillus in the north-east quadrant.

Other easily seen craters are the deep, circular *Reinhold* and *Landsberg* (both about 50 km, 30 mi dia) south-west of Copernicus, and the very fine *Eratosthenes* (65 km, 40 mi) on the edge of the Apennines, north-east of Copernicus.

OTHER FEATURES

The mountain ranges bordering the Mare Imbrium are the most interesting other features in this quadrant, particularly the *Apennines*, which soar to some 6000 metres (20,000 ft); the *Alps*, which peak at Mont Blanc (3600 metres, 12,000 ft) at the southern end of the Alpine Valley; and the *Carpathians* (up to 2100 metres, 7000 ft).

Also interesting are individual and groups of isolated peaks in the Mare Imbrium. South of Plato is the 2400-metre (7900-ft) *Mt Pico*, close to which is a group of peaks known as the *Teneriffe Mountains*. West of them is the curious *Straight Range*, which lies east-west. Another low but easily recognised ridge, the *Spitzbergen Mountains*, to the north of Archimedes, points north-south.

The Solar System

In 1543, Nicolaus Copernicus put Man's corner of the universe in perspective by proposing a solar system – a system in which the Sun is the dominant body and Earth is a mere planet orbiting around the Sun. And the Sun is indeed dominant. Seven hundred and fifty times more massive than all the rest of the matter in the solar system put together, it is able, by its immense gravitational pull, to hold in check tiny bodies like Pluto at a distance of 6000 million km (3700 million mi). Besides the nine planets, the Sun's family includes over 50 satellites of the planets, thousands of minor planets, or asteroids, and innumerable comets and meteoroids. In recent years, this family has been increased by hundreds of artificial Earth satellites and space probes launched by Man.

Relative sizes of the planets, shown in order from left to right going out from the Sun with their orbits drawn to scale.

Sun

DATA ON THE PLANETS

Planet	Mean distance from Sun (×10⁶)		Equatorial diameter		Density (water =1)	Circles Sun in:	Turns on axis in:
	(km)	(miles)	(km)	(miles)			
Mercury	58	36	4878	3032	5·4	88d	59d
Venus	108	67	12,104	7523	5·2	224·7d	243d
Earth	150	93	12,756	7926	5·52	365·25d	23:56h
Mars	228	142	6794	4222	3·95	687d	24:37h
Jupiter	778	484	142,800	88,750	1·34	11·9y	9:50h
Saturn	1427	887	120,000	74,580	0·70	29·5y	10:14h
Uranus	2870	1783	52,000	32,000	1·58	84·0y	17h
Neptune	4497	2794	48,400	30,100	2·30	164·8y	18h
Pluto	5900	3670	2200	1300	?	247·7y	153h

The Planets

The most important members of the solar system are the planets. Their name means 'wanderer', for to the eye they appear to be stars wandering around the celestial sphere, quite unlike the other 'fixed' stars. Unlike the stars, which never appear as more than points of light, each planet (except for Pluto) presents a measurable disc in the telescope. The planets are not self-luminous bodies like the stars, but shine by reflected light. Because of this, the nearer ones show distinct phases.

The planets vary widely in size and nature. Jupiter, Saturn, Uranus and Neptune are so much larger than the rest that they are termed *giant* or *major* planets. The rest are termed *terrestrial* planets, because they bear resemblances to Earth. For example, whereas the giant planets are predominantly gaseous and have many satellites, the terrestrial planets are composed of rock and have few if any satellites. The behaviour of the planets in the heavens makes it sensible to divide them in another way – into *inferior* and *superior* planets. The terms refer respectively to those inside (Mercury and Venus) and those outside (Mars, Jupiter, Saturn, Uranus, Neptune and Pluto) the Earth's orbit.

Planets move around the Sun in elliptical orbits, a fact first stated by Kepler in 1609 as his first law of planetary motion. Because the orbital path is an ellipse, the distance between the planet and the Sun varies throughout the orbit. When closest to the Sun, a planet is said to be at *perihelion*; when farthest from the Sun it is at *aphelion*. Most planetary orbits do not deviate much from a circle. Mercury and Pluto, though, do have much more eccentric orbits. Because of the great range of distances between the planets and the Sun, orbital periods vary widely, from 88 days for Mercury to nearly 250 years for Pluto.

Symbols of the planets

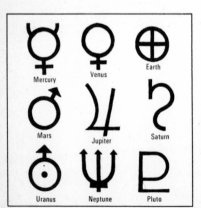

Signs of the constellations of the zodiac.

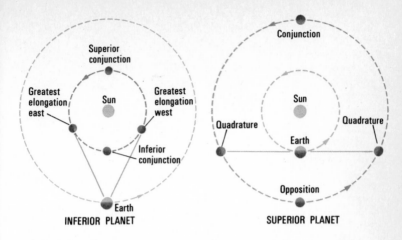

Significant positions in the orbits of an inferior planet (left) and a superior planet (right) as viewed from the Earth.

These two planets are also exceptional in wandering far from the plane of the ecliptic – the Sun's apparent path through the heavens. The planes of their orbits are inclined respectively at some 17° and 7° compared with about 3° and less for the others. With the exception of Pluto, the planets move within the imaginary band in the heavens known as the *zodiac*, which extends about 9° on each side of the ecliptic. The relative positions of the planets in the 12 zodiacal constellations – Aries, Taurus, Gemini, Cancer, Leo, Virgo, Libra, Scorpius, Sagittarius, Capricornus, Aquarius and Pisces – have profound significance in the pseudo-science of astrology.

Another fundamental motion of the planets is their axial rotation – they spin on their axes like tops while they travel around the Sun. With the exception of Mercury, Venus and Jupiter, the axes of rotation of the planets are appreciably inclined to the planes of their orbits around the Sun. The Earth's axis is inclined at $23\frac{1}{2}°$ to the vertical, and it is this tilt that accounts for the seasons (page 89). The axis of Uranus is inclined over 90° and lies nearly in the plane of the planet's orbit.

The planets, when viewed from the north of the solar system, orbit the Sun in an anticlockwise direction. Most satellites also orbit around their parent planets anticlockwise. But a few, for example the small outer moons of Jupiter, orbit clockwise, or in a *retrograde* direction. When it comes to planetary axial rotation, the norm is also anticlockwise. Only Venus and Uranus have a retrograde action.

Viewed from the Earth, the motion of the planets through the heavens is far from straightforward. This is because the Earth itself is moving in relation to the planets. It periodically catches up and overtakes the other planets, making them appear to perform intriguing loops in the sky. A diagram of what happens with superior planets is shown on page 93. It explains how they display retrograde motion around opposition.

The Inner Planets

Sun

Venus

The planets that lie within the Earth's orbit – Mercury and Venus – present problems for the telescopic observer. Mercury is too small and too distant for its surface to be observed; Venus is constantly wreathed in clouds so its surface is permanently obscured; and neither moves far away from the Sun, as viewed from the Earth.

Both planets are seen as morning stars in the east just before sunrise or as evening stars in the west at sunset. There is no mistaking Venus which shines like a beacon in the darkening sky. Mercury is much more elusive and never rises far above the horizon. It is best seen near the time of greatest elongation, when it may attain a brightness of magnitude $-1·2$. Venus reaches its maximum brightness (mag $-4·4$) about a month on either side of inferior conjunction. It is then the brightest object in the sky apart from the Sun and the Moon. It may even cast shadows. Whereas Mercury appears pinkish, Venus is brilliant white.

Like the Moon, Mercury and Venus show phases. But unlike the Moon, they appear to change in size as they journey in their orbit. They are smallest at full phase, which occurs at superior conjunction, and largest, but invisible, at 'new' phase, which occurs at inferior conjunction.

Occasionally, Mercury and Venus move directly in front of the Sun, as viewed from the Earth, this being known as a *transit*.

Above: A crescent Venus.

Top right: The surface of Mercury, as pictured by the Mariner 10 probe.

Below: The rocky surface of Venus, photographed by the Venera 10 probe.

PROFILE OF THE PLANETS (Data on page 83)

The second smallest of the major planets, Mercury, is closest to the Sun. On its sunlit side, which is exposed (because of its slow rotation) for days on end to the Sun's heat, temperatures soar to nearly 400°C, yet they plummet to nearly −200°C on the dark side. Like that of Pluto, Mercury's orbit is notably eccentric. The planet approaches within 47 million km of the Sun at perihelion yet is over 69 million km distant at aphelion (29 and 43 million miles).

Little surface detail is evident through telescopes, and the first close-up look at the planet did not come until 1974, when the space probe Mariner 10 flew by it. The surface looks almost identical to that of some parts of the Moon. It is heavily cratered, and there are also smoother regions resembling lunar maria. The crust appears to be of similar composition to the Moon's and reflects about the same amount (7%) of sunlight. Unexpectedly, a slight magnetic field was detected, together with the merest hint of a helium atmosphere.

There is no mere hint about the atmosphere of Venus, however. It is incredibly dense, and the atmospheric pressure at the surface appears to be 100 times that on Earth. The atmosphere is almost entirely composed of carbon dioxide. There are also traces of water vapour, and the clouds may be made up of sulphuric acid droplets. The atmosphere has a four-day circulation, totally at variance with the very slow (243-day) rotation of the planet itself. The ultradense atmosphere acts like a greenhouse and traps the Sun's heat, sending temperatures soaring to 450°C or more.

Spacecraft which have landed on Venus, including the Venera 9 and 10 probes, showed a rocky basaltic crust. Radar observations from the Earth and from the orbiting Magellan spacecraft have revealed both impact craters and lofty volcanoes on the surface that is criss-crossed with scars and fractures.

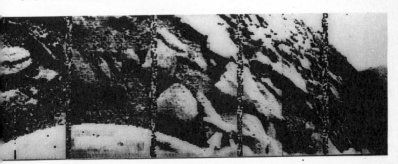

Planet Earth

Left: The Earth from space, snapped by the Apollo 17 astronauts. Below: Volcanic activity shows that the Earth is still evolving.

Earth has several features in common with other planets. It orbits in a similar plane and its axis is tilted. Its density is similar to that of Mercury and Venus. But it possesses many attributes that make it unique in the solar system. The primary one, of course, is that it supports an abundance of different life forms. Life is possible because of a happy combination of the planet's size and its location in the solar system.

Because of its size, Earth has been able to retain an appreciable atmosphere. This atmosphere contains oxygen, which all known plants and animals must breathe to live; it serves as a blanket to retain heat at night; and it contains an ozone layer which filters out dangerous ultraviolet radiation from the Sun. The location of the Earth means that its temperatures are not too cold for life processes to occur nor too hot for organic molecules to break down.

Another unique feature of our planet is the presence of water in its liquid state, one more essential requirement for life. Water covers over two-thirds of the surface and has been one of the prime agents in shaping the Earth's surface. The other great shaper of the landscape has been tectonic activity – movement of the Earth's crust on the underlying mantle of fluid rock (see page 90). Movement of the crustal segments or plates, causes continental drift, sets off earthquakes, makes volcanoes erupt, and builds mountains.

The weather, vulcanism, erosion and plant life all combine to make the Earth's surface varied and beautiful, quite different from the barren, dusty and cratered wastelands of the Moon and nearby planets.

THE SEASONS

No matter where you live on Earth, there is a seasonal change in the climate. The change becomes more marked the farther you go away from the equator. Middle latitudes experience the four seasons of spring, summer, autumn and winter.

The seasons come about because of the inclination ($23\frac{1}{2}°$) of the Earth's axis to the plane of its orbit. If the axis were not inclined, the climate for a particular latitude would never change since the angle of the Sun on a particular point on Earth would not vary. But since the Earth's axis is inclined, the seasonal climatic changes do occur.

The diagram illustrates the four distinct stages in the Earth's orbit. On about December 21, the axis is tilted so that the north pole is inclined most away from the Sun and the south pole is inclined most towards the Sun. In the southern hemisphere, the Sun climbs to its highest point in the sky, and it is mid-summer. In the northern hemisphere, the Sun is at its lowest, and it is mid-winter. Viewed in relation to the celestial sphere, the Sun reaches its most southerly point on this date and appears to 'stand still' before journeying northwards. This date is known as the winter solstice (*solstice* meaning 'Sun standing still'). In a similar way, six months later, on about June 21, the situation is reversed, with the north pole being tilted most towards the Sun and the south pole most away from it. It is mid-summer (summer solstice) in the northern hemisphere and mid-winter in the southern.

Roughly midway between the summer and winter solstices there occur times, the *equinoxes*, when the Earth's axis is tilted neither towards nor away from the Sun. At these times day and night are of equal length everywhere on Earth. On about March 21 comes the vernal, or spring equinox, and on about September 23, the autumnal equinox.

EARTH DATA

Equatorial diameter:	12,756 km, 7926 mi
Polar diameter:	12,714 km, 7900 mi
Surface area:	5.1×10^8 km² 2×10^8 mi²
Volume:	1.1×10^6 km³ 2.6×10^5 mi³
Mean density:	5.52 (water = 1)
Mass:	6×10^{21} tonnes
Mean distance from Sun:	149,600,000 km 93,000,000 mi
Mean solar day:	24 hr
Sidereal day:	23 hr 56 min 4 sec
Sidereal year:	365.26 solar days
Speed in orbit:	29.8 km/sec 18.5 mi/sec
Escape velocity:	11.2 km/sec 7 mi/sec

Vernal equinox

Summer solstice

Winter solstice

March 21

June 21

December 21

September 23

Autumnal equinox

ANATOMY OF THE EARTH

Erosion is a major sculptor of the Earth. The Grand Canyon (above) resulted from aeons of erosion by water.

The diagram below outlines what the Earth's interior is thought to be like. A thin crust 'floats' on a deep mantle of semi-fluid rock, which surrounds a dense, liquid metal core. The circulation of the core is thought to be the source of the Earth's magnetic field. The core is layered, as is the mantle — probably basic silicate rock.

The crust beneath the oceans is much thinner than that beneath the continents. It consists primarily of dark basic basalt. On top of the basalt beneath the continents is another layer of lighter-coloured acidic granite. Near the surface, the bedrock is folded and contorted by the pressure of Earth movements. Basalt and granite are examples of fire-formed, or *igneous* rocks. When such rocks penetrate to the surface they are gradually broken down by erosion, and the fragments are transported away, usually by water, and deposited as a sediment. As aeons go by these sediments become compressed into rock — *sedimentary* rock (such as chalk and shale). Both igneous and sedimentary rocks may undergo remelting when they come into contact with intruding hot magma (molten rock). They recrystallize and reform as *metamorphic* rock (such as marble and slate).

Commonest among the minerals that make up the Earth's crust are silicon dioxide (silica, sand), aluminium oxide, and iron oxide. Oxygen (46%) and silicon (28%) are by far the most plentiful elements in the Earth's crust.

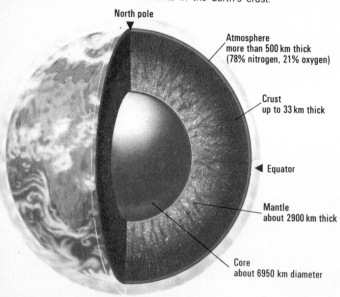

North pole

Atmosphere
more than 500 km thick
(78% nitrogen, 21% oxygen)

Crust
up to 33 km thick

◀ Equator

Mantle
about 2900 km thick

Core
about 6950 km diameter

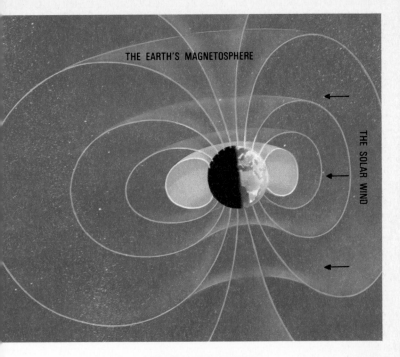

THE EARTH'S MAGNETOSPHERE

THE SOLAR WIND

EARTH PHENOMENA

Aurora Observers of the heavens in high latitudes north and south are regularly treated to one of Earth's most spectacular phenomena – the aurora. In the northern hemisphere, it is called the *aurora borealis*, or northern lights; in the southern hemisphere, the *aurora australis*, or southern lights. During an auroral display the night sky is lit up with arcs, streamers and shimmering folds of coloured light. At times the aurora may be visible in mid-latitudes, but there it usually appears as a general glow. Auroral displays occur when charged particles emitted from the Sun ionize the gases in the upper atmosphere and stimulate them to glow.

Gegenschein Also called counterglow. An oval patch of light in the heavens diametrically opposite the position of the Sun. It can best be seen on very dark moonless nights. It is thought to be caused by sunlight being scattered by dust particles in the plane of the ecliptic.

Magnetosphere The magnetic envelope surrounding the Earth in space, shown in the diagram above. It is not symmetrical because of the effect of the solar wind – it is 'dented' on the side towards the Sun and is elongated on the other side. The charged particles in the solar wind – protons and electrons – become trapped by the magnetic lines of force and are thereby prevented from reaching the Earth's surface. The particles congregate into two doughnut-shaped belts, the Van Allen belts, which are sources of intense radiation. Polar regions are the Achilles heel of the magnetosphere, for there the particles can penetrate without being deflected.

Zodiacal light A faint cone of light seen in the west after sunset and in the east before sunrise. It is sunlight that has been scattered by dust in the plane of the ecliptic. It is best seen in the tropics; in mid-latitudes it is more likely to be observed in the spring after sunset, or in the autumn just before dawn.

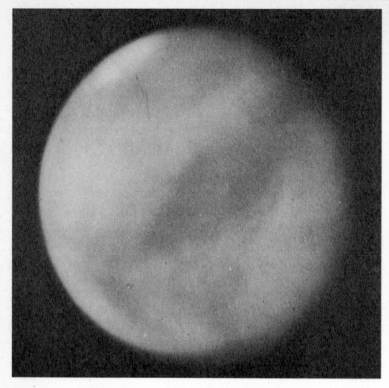

Mars – the Red Planet

Mars, probably the most intriguing of the planets, shines with a distinctive reddish-orange hue. At favourable oppositions it reaches a magnitude of nearly -2.5 and outshines even Jupiter. Oppositions of Mars occur every 26 months but, because of the planet's eccentric orbit, opposition distances vary from 100 million km (62 million mi) when it is at aphelion to only 56 million km (35 million mi) when it is at perihelion (the Earth's orbit is more or less circular). The most favourable oppositions, at perihelion, occur every 15 years or so, the next being in 1986. But even at the least favourable oppositions, Mars is brighter than mag -1.

Like all the superior planets, Mars exhibits retrograde motion in the heavens around opposition. Normally it travels eastwards across the celestial sphere, but near opposition it begins to travel westwards before resuming its easterly course. The diagram explains how this occurs; because the Earth is travelling faster in its orbit, it starts to catch up with and finally overtakes Mars, making the planet appear to backtrack for a while. The path of retrogression varies from planet to planet. Mars performs a loop, rather like a written *e*, as does Jupiter. Saturn and Uranus, on the other hand, retrogress along their own paths, that is, in a straight line. It is this apparently odd behaviour of the planets which confused the ancient astronomers. They resorted to systems of deferents and epicycles in an endeavour to explain it.

Unlike Venus, Mars does reveal some surface features through a telescope, though they appear vague in all except the largest instruments. Ice caps can be seen in polar regions, and dark areas elsewhere. The aspect of these markings appears to change as the planet rotates, in a little over $24\frac{1}{2}$ hours. Both the polar caps and the dark markings change with the Martian seasons – which are nearly twice as long as Earth's because the Martian year is nearly two Earth-years long. Sometimes, changes occur in the planet's appearance that even the naked eye can detect. In 1956 and 1971, for example, great planet-wide dust storms made Mars look paler.

More is known about Mars than about any other planet, since it has been comprehensively surveyed by space probes in orbit and on the surface. It has long been regarded as the planet most likely to harbour life of some sort, but this now seems most unlikely.

Diagram showing how Mars retrogresses.

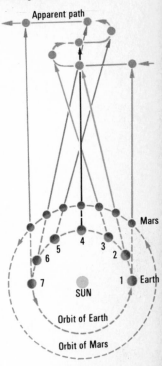

Top left: Through a powerful telescope ice caps and dark markings can be seen on Mars.
Right: Nix Olympica, the giant Martian volcano.
Below: The Martian surface, pictured by Viking.

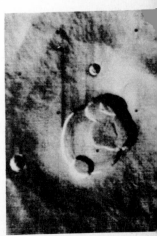

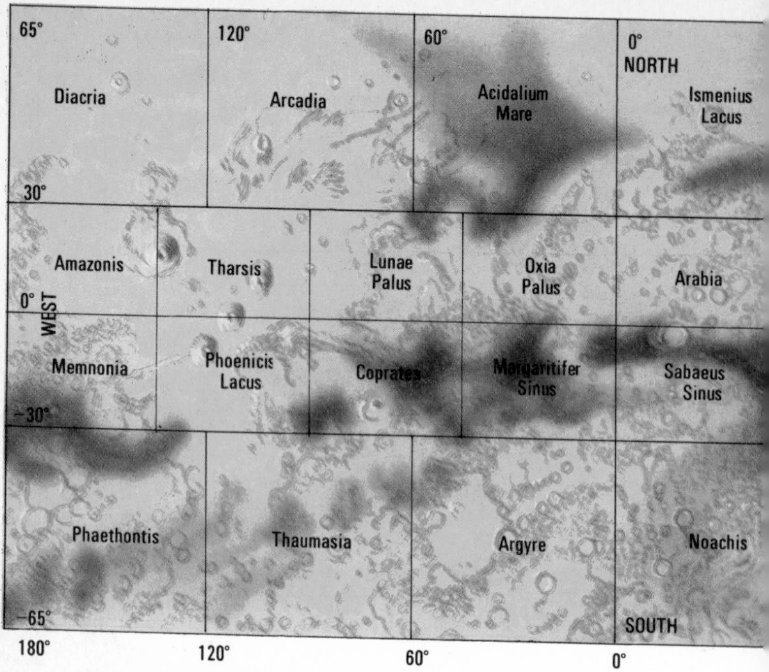

65°	120°	60°	0° NORTH
Diacria	Arcadia	Acidalium Mare	Ismenius Lacus
Amazonis	Tharsis	Lunae Palus	Oxia Palus	Arabia
Memnonia	Phoenicis Lacus	Coprates	Margaritifer Sinus	Sabaeus Sinus
Phaethontis	Thaumasia	Argyre	Noachis

180°   120°   60°   0°

PROFILE OF MARS
(Data on page 83)

Mars is very much smaller than the Earth, about half the diameter and a tenth of the mass. But its rotational period is very similar and it, too, experiences seasons because of its almost identical axial tilt (24°). It naturally has a much lower surface gravity than the Earth, and has been able to retain only a vestige of an atmosphere. The gases that remain are predominantly carbon dioxide, together with small amounts of nitrogen and argon. There are also slight traces of water vapour. Because the atmosphere is so thin the surface temperature varies widely between day, when it may rise above freezing, and night, when it may plummet to −200°C or below. Because of its eccentric orbit there are also great seasonal changes in surface temperature.

The prominent polar ice caps, once thought to be frozen carbon dioxide, are almost certainly water ice. This has become apparent from temperature studies of the polar regions and from the appearance of the caps in close-up photographs. These close-ups have been taken in recent years by a series of American Mariner and Viking probes which have scanned the planet from orbit. Detailed maps of the Martian surface have been compiled from these photographs. The projection shown above is based upon them. Shading is superimposed to match the dark regions observed telescopically from Earth.

Viewed from orbit, the Martian surface shows astonishing variety. There are many regions reminiscent of a lunar landscape, pockmarked with craters large and small. There are jumbled, 'chaotic' regions the like of which has never been seen anywhere else. There are relatively smooth regions (such as Hellas) resembling lunar mare areas. There is a vast canyon, a great scar-like fault up to 80 km (50 mi) wide that stretches for 5000 km (3000 mi). There are three massive volcanoes on the high Tharsis Ridge, and an even larger

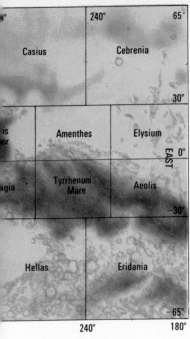

	240°	65°
Casius	Cebrenia	
		30°
is or	Amenthes	Elysium
		0° EAST
gia	Tyrrhenum Mare	Aeolis
		-30°
Hellas	Eridania	
		-65°
240°		180°

one nearby, Nix Olympica. This soars to a height of 30 km (20 mi) from a base 500 km (300 mi) across.

Of particular interest are the channels which look much like watercourses that can be seen in many regions. Most astronomers are convinced that they were made by water. They believe that water was once abundant on Mars, perhaps locked as ice in the ground until released as a flood when the ice was melted by volcanic activity or meteoritic impact.

There is no evidence of the celebrated 'canals', or linear features that the astronomer Schiaparelli reported he observed on Mars, thereby giving rise to theories of a Martian civilization. And the 'wave of darkening' that occurs during spring, once thought to be due to the growth of vegetation, is now considered to be caused by the global shift of surface dust by winds in the atmosphere. Dust storms have been observed on Mars from orbit as well as from Earth. And there is plenty of evidence of dust in the close-up

pictures taken by the Viking landers, which soft landed on Mars in 1976.

These probes sent back astonishingly good pictures, which showed a generally rocky landscape of what appear to be volcanic rocks in fine sand. The whole landscape has a deep red-orange tint, due to the presence of iron superoxide. Soil analysers in the lander, which carried out tests for life processes, reported puzzling results. At first it appeared that some kind of organic life was present, but it soon became clear that what was being revealed was a peculiar kind of chemistry in the surface materials. This does not mean, of course, that there is no life on Mars. But it adds to the mounting evidence which suggests that Martian life is mere wishful thinking.

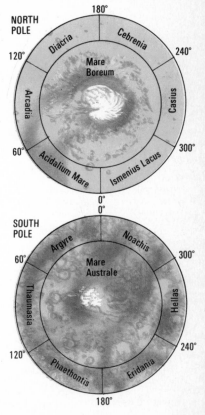

Twin Giants

The giants of the solar system, Jupiter and Saturn, are perhaps the most rewarding of the planets to observe. Though they are thought to be quite similar as planets – in composition, for example – they look quite different.

Jupiter is a brilliant object which even binoculars will reveal as a distinct disc. At oppositions, which occur every 13 months, it reaches a magnitude of between −2·3 and −2·5 (most favourable). Then it vies with Mars to be the brightest planet after Venus, though, being brilliant white, it can readily be distinguished from the red planet. On occasion, Mars and Jupiter reach opposition at about the same time in the same part of the heavens, affording an opportunity for fascinating viewing and comparisons. This happened, for example, in December-January 1977/8 in the constellation Gemini. The night-by-night movements of the two planets could be clearly traced by reference to the immobile stellar twins Castor and Pollux. By comparison, Saturn is rather a disappointing naked-eye and binocular object, seldom exceeding mag −0·2 at opposition.

Even a low-powered telescope will reveal the broad details of Jupiter's disc. It is seen to consist of alternate, roughly parallel, light and dark

Left: Jupiter as seen through a telescope on Earth, showing the prominent cloud belts in its atmosphere.
Right: Jupiter again, snapped by the Pioneer 11 probe in 1974.
Below: The gem of the solar system, the beautiful ringed planet Saturn.

bands; the light ones are known as *zones* and the dark ones *belts*. These features are not fixed but change regularly as the planet rotates in a little under 10 hours. They appear to be clouds in the thick Jovian atmosphere that have been forced into a band formation by the rapid rotation of the planet. Other features appear on and disappear from the surface sporadically. The most persistent of these has been the Great Red Spot, an oval red patch in the southern hemisphere which has been observed on and off since 1664.

When a low-powered telescope is turned on Saturn, little detail of the zones and belts of its disc can be made out. But the observer will not be disappointed because he will see one of the most beautiful sights in astronomy – Saturn's rings. The system of rings girdles the planet's equator and consists of two bright outer rings, separated by a dark (Cassini) division, and one faint and one very faint inner ring (the crêpe ring). Because of the inclination of Saturn's axis, the aspect of the rings changes noticeably year by year during the planet's 30-year orbital period.

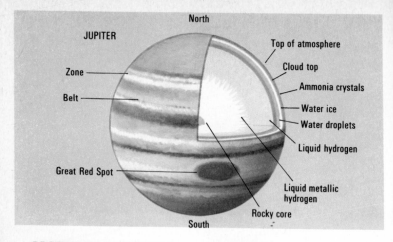

North

JUPITER

Top of atmosphere

Zone

Cloud top

Belt

Ammonia crystals

Water ice

Water droplets

Liquid hydrogen

Great Red Spot

Liquid metallic
hydrogen

Rocky core

South

PROFILE OF THE GIANTS
(Data on page 83)

Larger by far than the other planets, Jupiter and Saturn are thought to be very similar in composition. More is known about Jupiter because it has been surveyed in recent years by space probes such as Pioneers 10 and 11 and Voyagers 1 and 2. The planet is made up predominantly of hydrogen, which exists as gas in a 1000-km (600-mi) deep atmosphere. Beneath the atmosphere there is thought to be a 24,000-km (15,000-mi) layer of liquid hydrogen and beneath that a 46,000-km (29,000-mi) layer of dense liquid metallic hydrogen around a possible small rocky core.

The liquid metallic hydrogen is thought to exist under a pressure of three million atmospheres and at a temperature of some 11,000°C. Internal temperatures in Jupiter are thought to rise to some 30,000°C. There is evidence of such high temperatures in the fact that Jupiter radiates two to three times the amount of energy it receives from the Sun.

Because the planet is essentially fluid, its rapid rotation causes marked flattening at the poles, where the radius is nearly 5000 km (3000 mi) less than that at the equator. The rapid rotation also causes the marked banding of the clouds. The light zones appear to be higher and cooler than the dark belts. The Great Red Spot, which is up to

about 40,000 km (25,000 mi) long and 14,000 km (9000 mi) wide, appears to be a persistent storm — a gigantic Jovian hurricane.

Jupiter is unique among the planets in being a radio emitter, the radiation appearing to come from the motion of high-speed electrons trapped in the planet's exceedingly strong magnetic field. Some bursts of radiation are triggered off by the passage of the large, close-orbiting satellite Io.

Io is a fascinating body which has a slight atmosphere and reddish polar caps. It is surrounded by an ionized cloud of sodium, which bathes the planet in a yellow glow. Of the other three large Jovian planets, Europa is a rocky body covered with ice and frost, while Ganymede, the largest of all satellites, may well be mostly liquid water with an icy crust. Callisto, too, could be partly liquid water.

The main globe of Saturn is more or less a pale imitation of that of Jupiter. The polar regions are markedly flattened; cloud belts and zones are present but are not as obvious as Jupiter's. Transient spots and markings come and go but are not as easily identifiable as Jupiter's, nor are they so persistent.

But it is the flat ring system in Saturn's equatorial plane that makes the planet a unique spectacle. Three rings can clearly be seen. The outer one is about 16,000 km (10,000 mi) wide

1980

1988

1995

2002

and is separated from the brighter 26,000 km (16,000 mi) wide middle ring by the dark Cassini division, which is some 2600 km (1600 mi) wide. The faint inner, or crêpe ring is about 16,000 km (10,000 km) wide. Voyager photographs have resolved the whole ring system into thousands of very narrow threads, some of them intertwined or 'braided'.

From one edge to the other, the ring system extends for about 275,000 km (170,000 mi). Though it is wide, it is so thin that it practically disappears when viewed edge-on. Accurate measurements of the thickness of the rings made by Voyager 2 indicate that the rings are only about 100 metres thick. The individual ringlets are probably made up of icy 'snowballs', perhaps mixed with dust, up to a few metres across, fragments becoming detached and collecting together again as they orbit Saturn.

Left: Different aspects of the rings come into view during Saturn's year. Below: The surface of Saturn's big moon Titan could look like this. It is one of the few moons to have an atmosphere.

Far-distant Worlds

Saturn is the remotest of the planets known to the ancient astronomers. Beyond it lie Uranus, found by William Herschel in 1781; Neptune, found by J. G. Galle in 1846; and Pluto, found by Clyde Tombaugh as recently as 1930. Uranus and Neptune, although considerably larger than the Earth, are so far away that little detail can be seen on their discs even in large-aperture telescopes. They can, however, be readily found and followed through the heavens even with binoculars, using a current astronomical almanac for reference. Uranus can reach nearly mag 5 and Neptune, mag 8.

In large-aperture telescopes Uranus presents a greenish disc on which twin equatorial belts may just be distinguished. These belts lie almost perpendicular to the orbital plane because of the great inclination (98°) of the planet's axis of rotation. In 1977 it was discovered that Uranus, like Saturn, possessed a ring system around its equator, but it is much too faint to be observed from Earth. Neptune shows a suggestion of cloud belts on its bluish disc but nothing definite can be discerned even with the largest instruments. Both Uranus and Neptune appear to be gaseous planets similar to Jupiter and Saturn in make-up. They have thick atmospheres of hydrogen and methane. They are both very cold, Uranus being close to −200°C and Neptune being about 20° colder.

Pluto is so tiny and so far away that very little is known about it. For most of its 248-year, highly eccentric orbit Pluto is the most remote planet, but for 20 years or so (for example, between 1979–1999) it actually curves inside Neptune's orbit. Astronomers think it is probably a terrestrial-type planet. It may be covered with frozen methane gas at a temperature of −225°C. If so, it would be highly reflective. Satellite Charon, discovered in 1978, may be half as big as Pluto itself.

Above: Neptune pictured with its two moons (arrowed) – Triton and the distant Nereid.

Right: Uranus and its five satellites.

Below: Close inspection of star photographs is needed to reveal the presence of the tiny planet Pluto.

BEYOND PLUTO

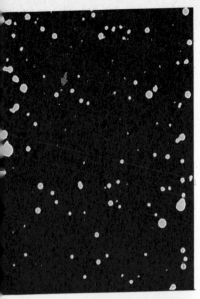

Pluto was really found by chance. Astronomer Percival Lowell predicted where it should be in the heavens according to calculations he made as a result of observed irregularities, or perturbations, in the orbit of Neptune. Eventually, it was found exactly as predicted. But it is now recognized that Pluto itself is too insignificant to cause the observed perturbations. Is there then another planet, or planets, waiting to be discovered?

Though no-one can be certain, it seems possible that there could be. Computer studies have suggested that a planet three times more massive than Saturn could orbit in a retrograde direction (clockwise) at a distance of 10,000 million km (6000 million miles) from the Sun. The chances of finding such an object, if it indeed exists, are very slim since it must be very faint. But a chance occultation by planet X of a star under observation could lead to its discovery.

It is extremely unlikely that the Sun is the only star in the universe to have a family of planets circling it. There is not much doubt that there are many 'solar systems' in space. There does seem to be evidence of planetary systems around two of the nearer stars, Barnard's Star and ε Eridani. The former is a red dwarf with only one-seventh the mass of the Sun, while the latter is a yellow dwarf only slightly smaller than the Sun.

The systematic study of these two stars over long periods has revealed that they 'wobble' slightly as they move. Since they are relatively close to us (6 and 11 light-years), their proper motions can be detected. The observed wobble in their motions is interpreted as being due to the presence of encircling planets. The evidence points to there being two planets orbiting Barnard's Star, one with a mass close to that of Jupiter and another of about half that mass. This does not rule out the possibility of other planets, for their effect would be too small to be detected. The wobble of ε Eridani could be caused by a massive planet with six times Jupiter's mass. There is also evidence of 'wobble' in the motions of other relatively close stars.

Many Moons

Planet	*Larger known satellites	†Distance from planet (10⁻³km)	Diameter (km)
Earth	Moon	384	3476
Mars	Phobos	9	23
	Deimos	23	13
Jupiter	Io	422	3652
	Europa	671	2900
	Ganymede	1070	5000
	Callisto	1883	4500
Saturn	Mimas	186	390
	Enceladus	238	500
	Tethys	295	1050
	Dione	377	1120
	Rhea	527	1530
	Titan	1222	5120
	Hyperion	1483	290
	Iapetus	3560	1440
	Phoebe	12,950	140?
Uranus‡	Miranda	130	480
	Ariel	192	1170
	Umbriel	267	1190
	Titania	438	1590
	Oberon	586	1550
Neptune	Triton	355	2700
	Nereid	5562	340?
Pluto	Charon	19	1200

*In order of discovery †Mean distance
‡Uranus has 10 additional smaller moons

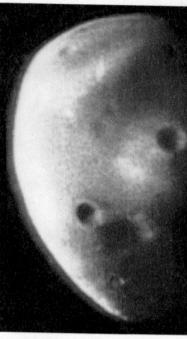

The Martian moon Deimos as revealed by a Viking Mars probe in 1976.

After the planets, the next largest bodies in the solar system are their satellites, or moons. The Earth has the Moon (page 64ff) as its only satellite. Mars has two satellites; Jupiter 16 or maybe more; Saturn 18; Uranus 15; and Neptune eight. Most interesting to the casual observer are the four brightest moons of Jupiter, which Galileo saw in 1609. They can easily be seen even in low-powered binoculars, when they are observed strung out in a line, since they all orbit in Jupiter's equatorial plane. With maximum magnitudes of 5–6, they would be naked-eye objects were it not for their proximity to their ultra-bright parent planet.

The largest Jovian moon, Ganymede, is bigger than the planet Mercury, as is the largest of Saturn's moons, Titan. Titan is interesting because it has an atmosphere that might be as thick as Earth's, though of different composition. Titan and Rhea, Saturn's next largest moon, are the only other satellites in the solar system brighter than the 10th magnitude.

The Asteroids

Circling in the great void between the orbits of Mars and Jupiter is a collection of rocky bodies called asteroids or minor planets. The majority of them, including the largest Ceres, orbit in a broad band known as the asteroid belt. A few, including Adonis, Icarus and Eros, wander farther afield.

Ceres was the first to be discovered, by Guiseppe Piazzi on 1 January, 1801. By 1807 three more had been discovered – Pallas, Juno and Vesta. By 1990 over 3500 asteroids had been named, and many more had been discovered although their orbits were not accurately calculated. Statistical estimates give the total number of asteroids larger than 1·5 km at nearly half a million.

Their total mass is estimated to be in the region of $2 \cdot 5 \times 10^{24}$g, or about four ten-thousandths of the mass of the Earth. This is strong evidence against the once-favoured theory that the asteroids are the remains of a tenth planet that broke up some time in the distant past. They undoubtedly originated during the formation of the rest of the solar system and some may indeed be made up of unchanged primeval materials.

It is only in recent years that the sizes of the asteroids have been accurately determined and in general they appear to be 30% bigger than was once thought (see table). They are probably all irregularly shaped bodies pitted with craters, somewhat like the Martian moons (see opposite). Some are known to be irregular from their light variation – for example, Eros, which has dimensions of about $7 \times 16 \times 35$ km. Several of the asteroids are bright enough to be visible in low-power instruments, and Vesta can at times just be seen with the naked eye.

Asteroids show up as streaks in long-exposure star photographs.

THE LARGEST ASTEROIDS

No	Name	Diameter (km)	*Distance from Sun (10^6 km)
1	Ceres	1000	420
2	Pallas	610	350
4	Vesta	540	350
10	Hygeia	450	470
31	Euphrosyne	370	470
704	Interamnia	350	460
511	Davida	330	480
65	Cybele	310	510
52	Europa	290	470
451	Patientia	280	460
15	Eunomia	270	400
16	Psyche	250	440

*Mean distance

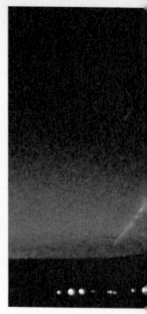

Comets

Bright comets are among the least predictable occurrences in the heavens. A few recorded examples have stretched halfway across the sky, and the head may even be visible in daylight.

Unfortunately, most of the comets that appear each year as their orbits bring them close to the Sun and the Earth are too faint to be seen with the naked eye. These are the short-period comets, which never recede beyond about the distance of Neptune. Their orbits are well known, and their returns are predictable. Encke's Comet, which orbits the Sun every 3·3 years, has the shortest period of all.

The best known of this group is Halley's Comet, which was last seen in 1986. It orbits the Sun every 76 years. It is named after Edmund Halley, who predicted the comet's orbit and was the first person to recognize that comets are members of the solar system.

The rare spectacular comets all belong to the long-period group. Their orbits are enormously elongated, and they travel to and from regions of the solar system far beyond Pluto in periods of thousands of years. Many astronomers believe that comets originate in matter lying in a shell some 200 million million kilometres from the Sun.

Although there have been few bright comets this century to rival those of the last (famous ones were seen in 1811, 1843, 1858 (Donati's), 1868 and 1882), the brilliant comets of 1965 (Ikeya-Seki) and 1976 (West) would have become legendary if the night skies over cities were still as dark as they were in the 19th century.

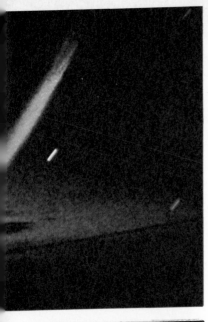

ANATOMY OF A COMET

A comet is thought to be composed of small rocks and dust particles cemented together by frozen gas and ice. For much of its orbit around the Sun it remains invisible, since it radiates no light of its own. Then, as the comet approaches the Sun it begins to glow as sunlight is reflected from it. The frozen gas begins to vaporize, releasing some of the dust.

As it gets nearer, the gas molecules and fine dust specks are 'blown', or repelled by the solar wind — the stream of charged particles coming from the Sun. The gas becomes ionized and starts to emit light of its own. With the reflecting dust particles, it forms a tail to the comet, always pointing away from the Sun.

In its most developed state, when it is approaching perihelion, a comet is observed to have a fuzzy head, or *coma*, and a trailing tail. Centred in the coma is a dense *nucleus*, wherein most of its matter is concentrated. As the comet swings away from the Sun after perihelion, the tail begins to precede it. The farther it recedes, the fainter it becomes and the shorter is its tail. Eventually it returns to the oblivion from which it came.

The composition of comets can be found by observing the spectra of the light their ionized gases emit. They are found to consist of compounds containing carbon, nitrogen, oxygen, hydrogen, sodium, iron and nickel.

Top left: Comet Humason, 1961.
Centre: Comet Ikeya-Seki, 1965.
Below: Halley's comet, 1910.

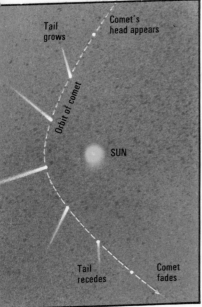

105

Meteors

This star trail picture shows a meteor track.

On most dark nights if you gaze at the heavens for a short while you are almost bound to see the bright streaks of light we know as meteors, or shooting stars. These streaks mark the passage of tiny rocky or metallic particles through the Earth's upper atmosphere. Travelling at relative speeds of up to 70 km/sec (45 mi/sec), these particles are heated to incandescence by air friction, and eventually burn up and disperse into fine dust. This happens at altitudes between about 80–120 km (50–75 mi).

For much of the year the meteors are sporadic, appearing from anywhere at any time. At some times, however, they become much more frequent and appear from a single direction as a meteor shower.

Normally the particles colliding with the atmosphere are not much larger than grains of sand. Occasionally, however, larger ones

METEOR SHOWERS

On an average night during the year about five or six meteors can be seen every hour. There are rather more after midnight, when the Earth's atmosphere encounters the meteoroid particles head on. At the time of meteor showers, however, the hourly rate increases dramatically to tens and very occasionally to hundreds. The showers occur regularly every year on or around the same dates and are caused by the Earth passing through the debris of broken-up comets. Because of perspective, the meteors in a shower all appear to originate from a point in the sky, which is termed the *radiant*. A shower is named after the constellation in which the radiant is located. Interesting showers include:

Quadrantids	Jan 1–5
April Lyrids	Apr 19–24
Aquarids	May 1–8
June Lyrids	Jun 10–21
Perseids	Jul 25–Aug 18
Cygnids	Aug 18–22
Orionids	Oct 16–27
Taurids	Oct 10–Dec 5
Leonids	Nov 14–20
Geminids	Dec 7–15

METEORITES

The Arizona meteorite crater shown right, known as Meteor Crater, is the largest on Earth, with a diameter of 1265 metres (4150 ft) and a depth of 175 metres (575 ft). The meteorite that caused it probably weighed up to 100,000 tonnes. Nothing remains of that meteorite, however. The largest so far found, at Hoba West in S.W. Africa, weighs nearly 60 tonnes.

Meteorites large and small are of two distinct types, mainly stony or mainly metallic. The stony types, or *aerolites*, are made up of silicates, while the metallic ones, or *siderites*, consist of an iron-nickel alloy of characteristic structure. When polished and etched, this structure shows up as a Widmanstätten pattern (see below).

appear, which announce their presence more spectacularly. They appear as a bright fireball, or bolide, often of vivid colour, and may be as large as the solar disc. They may leave a broad and persistent trail in their wake, and be accompanied by a sonic boom.

Witnessing a bolide is a matter of luck, since they cannot be predicted. Astronomically, it is an important event because it often results in fragments reaching the ground intact. If observers report bolides immediately, there is a chance of finding the fragments. Being of extraterrestrial origin, these fragments, or meteorites, make rewarding study. When very large meteorites hit the ground, huge craters are formed. The impact of meteorites seems to have been the main force that shaped the surface of the Moon and the planets Mercury and Mars, all of which are liberally dotted with craters.

The rim (above) of the Arizona crater (below).

The Sun

The star that breathes life into our planet is a very ordinary one. It has a diameter of 1,392,000 km (865,000 mi) – quite small by astronomical standards – and emits yellowish light. It is classed as a yellow dwarf of spectral type G2 and is in the Main Sequence on the Hertzsprung-Russell diagram (page 47). It is about 5000 million years old.

The Sun is composed mainly of hydrogen gas (93%), together with some helium (5%) and heavier elements (2%). It derives its energy from nuclear fusion reactions occurring in its core. Its light takes 8 minutes to traverse the 150 million km (93 million mi) to Earth. Light from the next nearest star takes over 4 years.

Like all heavenly bodies the Sun has two motions in space. First, it rotates on its axis like a top. The period of rotation at the equator is $25\frac{1}{3}$ days. The plane of rotation, as viewed from the Earth, changes during the

Above: Minutes after sunrise.
Below: The solar corona, from Skylab.

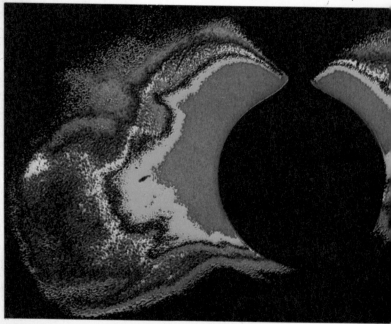

year because the Earth's axis is inclined to the plane of its orbit. Secondly, the Sun revolves around the centre of our Galaxy, some 30,000 light-years away; the period of revolution, the cosmic year, is 225 million years.

The Sun is by far the nearest star to Earth. Astronomers study it at every wavelength, from X-ray to radio wavelengths. It is a powerful emitter of radio waves. Because the Sun's disc is so bright, it is dangerous to look at it directly through a telescope. It is best to project the image on to a white surface and examine it there. The Sun's visible surface, or photosphere, is in constant turmoil; searing hot gas ripples over it and erupts into the solar atmosphere. Huge dark sunspots can often be seen on the disc, moving as the Sun rotates.

The solar atmosphere can normally be observed from Earth only fleetingly during solar eclipses, when the Moon's disc blots out the Sun's bright light, but astronomers can observe it regularly using satellites. The most important of these was the Solar Max satellite, which lasted from 1980 to 1989. It observed the corona and prominences, recorded 10,000 flares, and discovered 10 'sungrazing' comets. It also observed the fact that the Sun grows brighter during maximum sunspot activity. Solar Max could observe solar radiation from very short gamma-rays to long radio waves, and it is unique among satellites in having been repaired in orbit by a crew sent up in the Space Shuttle *Challenger* in 1984.

Cross-section of the Sun.

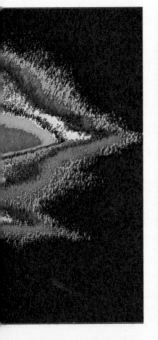

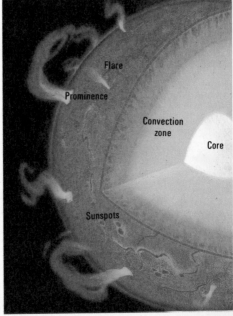

PROFILE OF THE SUN

Corona The outer atmosphere of the Sun, which becomes visible as a pearly halo during a total solar eclipse. It is very thin and gradually merges into space over a distance of several kilometres. Skylab observations showed that the corona is constantly changing as the condition of the solar surface changes.

Chromosphere The roughly 15,000-km (9000-mi) thick inner atmosphere of the Sun, which becomes visible as a rose-coloured ring during a total eclipse. The dark lines in the solar spectrum originate in the chromosphere, whose cool gas absorbs the wavelengths it would normally emit.

Eclipses By coincidence, the Moon is about 400 times smaller than the Sun in diameter, but is some 400 times closer, and it thus presents the same-size disc as the Sun. On occasions when the Moon moves between the Sun and the Earth, it blots out the Sun's light; this is an *eclipse of the Sun*. When the Moon's disc exactly covers that of the Sun, the eclipse is total for a few minutes (never more than about $7\frac{1}{2}$). Day turns into night as the Moon's shadow races across the Earth and

SUN DATA	
Equatorial diameter:	1,392,000 km
	865,000 mi
Volume:	1,303,600 Earth's volume
Mean density:	1·4 (water = 1)
Mass:	333,000 Earth's mass
Gravity:	28 Earth's gravity
Mean distance:	149,600,000 km
from Earth:	93,000,000 mi
Surface temperature:	6000°C
Core temperature:	ca 15,000,000°C
Spins on axis in:	25·4 days
Spectral type:	G2
Magnitude	
absolute:	4·8
apparent:	−26·7

sweeps out a path of total eclipse never more than about 250 km (150 mi) across. When the Moon's disc is not quite large enough to cover that of the Sun, an annular eclipse occurs, the dark Moon disc being surrounded by a bright ring.

Just before totality a phenomenon known as Baily's beads occurs; as beads of light peep through undulations on the lunar crust. A 'diamond-

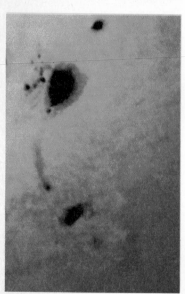

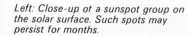

Above: Skylab astronauts took this picture of the Sun, which shows a giant prominence (bottom).

Left: Close-up of a sunspot group on the solar surface. Such spots may persist for months.

Features of an eclipse.

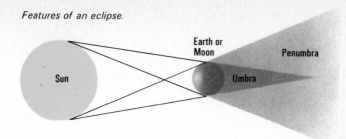

Sun

Earth or Moon

Penumbra

Umbra

ring' effect is also seen when only a tiny portion of the Sun remains uncovered.

The Earth, too, casts a shadow in space, and when the Moon passes into this shadow, an *eclipse of the Moon* occurs. Because the Moon is relatively small, it can remain in total eclipse for nearly two hours. When eclipsed, the Moon takes on a pale coppery hue due to its being illuminated by sunlight refracted onto it by the Earth's atmosphere.

Solar eclipses occur on average about two or three times a year; lunar eclipses once or twice a year. Eclipses occur in the same order at the same time every 18 years 11 days, a period (known to the ancients) called the *saros*.

Faculae Bright patches on the solar surface which seem to be connected with the appearance of sunspots.

Flares Sudden eruptions of very hot gas visible as intensely bright spots; associated with sunspots. They are the source of high-velocity charged particles that intensify the solar wind, disturb the Earth's ionosphere and cause spectacular aurorae.

Flocculi Also called *plages*; light and dark markings observed in monochromatic (one-colour, or single-wavelength) calcium or hydrogen light.

Fraunhofer lines The dark absorption lines in the solar spectrum, named after Joseph Fraunhofer (1787–1826), the German physicist who first investigated them thoroughly.

Fusion reactions The nuclear reactions that take place in the Sun's 15 million °C core, in which hydrogen atoms combine, or fuse into helium atoms. When this happens there is a slight loss in mass, which appears as energy according to Einstein's equation

$E = mc^2$, where E is the energy released by the conversion of mass m, and c is the velocity of light. Some 6000 million tonnes of hydrogen are consumed by the Sun every second to produce the 4×10^{20} MW of energy the Sun radiates.

Photosphere The visible part of the Sun's disc, from which solar radiation emanates. About 100 km (60 mi) thick, it has a temperature of about 6000°C.

Prominences Great streamers of hot glowing gas that erupt from the chromosphere and extend far into the corona before falling back. They can be viewed only during a total eclipse or in monochromatic light.

Solar wind The constant stream of charged particles – protons and electrons – that emanates from the Sun, which increases in intensity and velocity after eruptions on the solar surface.

Sunspots Dark patches on the solar disc that may cover an area of several thousand million square kilometres and may persist for many months. But most are smaller and shorter lived. A typical spot has a dark centre (umbra) and lighter surroundings (penumbra). It is about 2000°C cooler than the rest of the photosphere.

Sunspots come and go according to a fairly regular cycle of about 11 years. At times of sunspot maximum, the disc is seldom free from sunspots, while at minimum the disc can remain unblemished for months at a time. Practically all sunspots appear within 35° latitude north or south of the solar equator. After a sunspot minimum, spots usually appear in high latitudes, but as the cycle progresses the spots appear closer and closer to the solar equator. If the time spots appear is plotted against their latitude, the typical *butterfly diagram* appears.

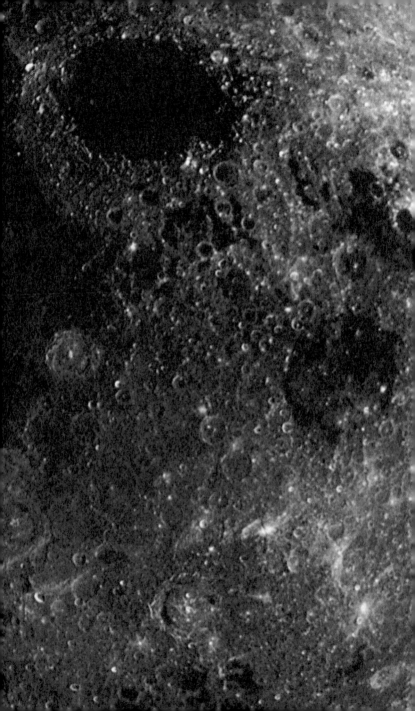

Telescopes

We can find out quite a bit about the heavens just by looking with the naked eye. But as an astronomical instrument the eye is far from ideal. Its great disadvantage is that it has a small aperture, or lens diameter, which severely limits its light-gathering power. The small aperture also reduces the eye's ability to resolve, or separate, stars that are close together.

Astronomers therefore have to rely on optical aid in the form of telescopes to increase light-gathering power and resolution. The two basic kinds of telescopes are the *refractor* and the *reflector*. The refractor gathers light by means of lenses, whereas the reflector uses a mirror. The light entering the telescope is gathered by the objective lens in a refractor or a curved mirror in the reflector, and brought to a focus. The image formed is then viewed by an eyepiece. In both refractor and reflector the image viewed is inverted, that is, upside-down. South is up and north is down; east to the right, west to the left.

The larger the diameter of the objective lens or mirror, the greater are the light-gathering power and resolution. The power increases as the square of the diameter, so a 100 mm diameter telescope will gather four times as much light as a 50 mm. Useful apertures for the amateur observer are from 75 mm (3 in) to 250 mm (10 in), the latter being able to detect stars as faint as the 14th magnitude and to resolve double stars 0·5 second of arc apart.

Power and resolution are more important attributes of a telescope than magnification. Magnification depends only on the ratio of the focal length of the objective to that of the eyepiece. Increasing the magnification will

Opposite: The Moon's surface viewed from lunar orbit.
Right: The dome of the 4-metre Mayall reflector at Kitt Peak Observatory in Arizona.

113

not increase light-gathering power or improve resolution. It will only make the images fainter, reduce the field of view, and magnify any disturbances or vibrations.

The most important thing about any telescope is the quality of its optical components. A telescope with poor optics will give a poor image no matter how big the aperture, and increasing the magnification will only increase the distortion. For the best-quality telescopes the useful magnification is limited to about twice the aperture in millimetres. So the useful limit of magnification for a 75 mm will be about × 150, and for a 100 mm, × 200. Using two or three different eyepieces will permit different magnifications. A low-power (long focal length) eyepiece is useful because it provides a large field of view, for observing comets, nebulae and similar extended objects.

The quality of viewing depends heavily on the state of the atmosphere at the time. The twinkling of the stars shows how the atmosphere can distort starlight. Rapid changes in temperature, breezy conditions, and

Eyepiece

Objective

The solar telescope at Mt Wilson Observatory.

REFRACTORS

The astronomical refractor has two optical components – an objective, or object glass at the front, and an ocular, or eyepiece at the rear, as shown above. The object glass is a convex, or converging lens system which brings the light rays it receives to a focus to form an image. The eyepiece, also a converging system, views and magnifies the image. It is mounted in a tube that slides in and out for focusing. Since the object glass has a long focal length, the telescope tube must be comparatively long to accommodate the lenses.

The object glass is not a simple lens, but a compound achromatic lens made up of two or more lenses of different types of glass. Achromatic lenses eliminate a basic defect of simple lenses – that of chromatic aberration. This defect occurs because light rays of different wavelengths take different paths as they are refracted into and out of the lens. It gives rise to a blurred, coloured image.

Big refracting telescopes are no longer made, because most professional astronomical research involves the study of faint objects requiring large apertures to reveal them well. It is much easier to build a very large mirror than a lens, and the world's largest refractor, the 1 metre aperture telescope at Yerkes Observatory, USA, was constructed a century ago.

In small sizes and for visual observation, refractors do have some advantages over reflectors since they often give sharper definition.

atmospheric pollution all impair viewing. To minimise these harmful effects, heavenly objects should be viewed as far from the horizon as possible. When they are near the horizon, their light has to pass through the greatest depth of atmosphere and suffers the greatest distortion. The quality of viewing conditions, termed *seeing*, should always be recorded during serious observational work. To record the quality of seeing, most observers use a scale devised by E. M. Antoniadi, of I (perfect viewing) to V (very poor).

The stability of the telescope during observation is another important factor. If it is inadequately supported, it is likely to pick up vibrations that again cause distortion of the image. Where possible, it is best to fix a telescope to a permanent pillar set in concrete. Where portability is required, a rigid heavy-duty pedestal should be used.

Most telescopes are fixed on their supports by an equatorial mounting. This permits the telescope to be turned so as to follow readily the motion of the stars through the heavens (see page 117). Following the stars becomes particularly important when photography is being used to record the telescopic image. With a time exposure, photographic film 'stores' starlight and can record very faint objects that the naked eye can never see. Charge-coupled devices (CCDs), used in video cameras, are rapidly replacing photography since they are far more sensitive to light and the 'picture' can be stored in a computer and processed to improve its quality. Increasing numbers of amateurs are also turning to 'video astronomy'.

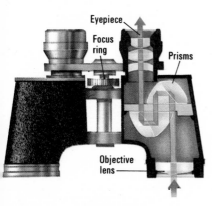

Eyepiece

Focus ring

Prisms

Objective lens

BINOCULARS

Binoculars are a kind of refracting telescope which use prisms to 'fold' the light path between object glass and eyepiece (see diagram). In this way the telescope tube can be made much shorter. For focusing, a pair of binoculars has a central adjuster, which moves both barrels in and out together.

Good instruments also have independent adjustment on one or both eyepieces. A good-quality instrument is essential for astronomical work where the optics of the system are being strained to their limits.

While binoculars do not have the magnification and resolving power of astronomical telescopes, they have two distinct advantages over their larger cousins. They give a bright image and they have a wide field of view. This makes them useful for such activities as watching comets, hunting for novae and observing scattered star clusters.

Binoculars are rated by their degree of magnification and their aperture diameter. Useful sizes for astronomical work are 7×50, 8×50, and 10×50, the first figure being the magnification and the second, the diameter of the object lens in millimetres. Some astronomical binoculars are very much bigger and much more powerful, such as 25×105, but they are not portable and must be mounted on a supporting stand. They are often used for comet hunting.

REFLECTORS

In an astronomical reflector the light rays are gathered by a parabolic concave mirror and reflected back up the telescope tube towards a secondary mirror. This secondary mirror then reflects the converging rays to a focus outside the telescope tube, where the image is examined by an eyepiece.

The main type of reflector used, the *Newtonian*, follows the layout Isaac Newton devised in 1672, when he constructed the first reflector. Its secondary mirror is flat and inclined at 45° to the telescope axis. It reflects the light it receives from the primary mirror through a right angle into the eyepiece, which is placed near the open end of the telescope tube. In the other main type, the *Cassegrain*, the secondary mirror is convex and reflects the light from the primary mirror back again down the telescope tube and through a hole in the primary mirror, where the eyepiece is located.

The Cassegrain has a longer focal length than the Newtonian and is more compact. But it has a narrower field and gives a fainter image. It is also more difficult and more expensive to construct. Most amateur astronomers use Newtonian reflectors. Large reflectors used in observatories are often fitted with alternative types of optical systems for use in different circumstances.

Reflectors are free from the chromatic aberration that plagues refractors. They also absorb less light, since the light rays do not pass through an object glass. They can be constructed in much larger sizes because the mirror can be supported from behind. The largest reflecting telescope with an orthodox primary mirror is the 6 metre telescope at Zelenchukskaya in the Caucasus, but the 10 metre aperture Keck reflector at Mauna Kea, Hawaii, consists of 36 separate hexagonal mirrors. Because the tube is so short, it takes up less space than the 5 metre Mount Palomar reflector, which was the world's largest from 1948 until 1976.

Though generally superior and cheaper to construct and buy than a refractor, a reflector does require more upkeep. The surface of the mirror, which consists of a thin aluminium coating on glass, must be well looked after and renewed regularly. And the optical components – the flat and the primary mirrors – must be precisely aligned. It is usually necessary to align them, or 'collimate the telescope' before observing.

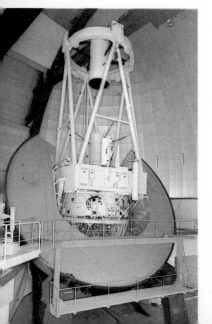

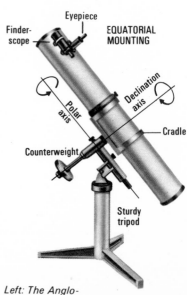

EQUATORIAL MOUNTING

Eyepiece

Finder-scope

Polar axis

Declination axis

Cradle

Counterweight

Sturdy tripod

Left: The Anglo-Australian 4-metre reflector.

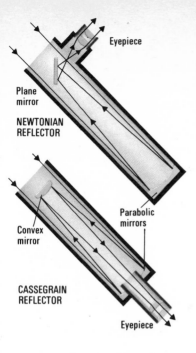

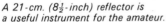
A 21-cm. (8½-inch) reflector is a useful instrument for the amateur.

MOUNTINGS

There are two basic methods of mounting a telescope on its support or pedestal. The simplest is the *altazimuth* mounting. This is similar to the 'pan-and-tilt' head of a camera tripod. It allows the telescope to be moved vertically or horizontally. In other words, the telescope can be moved in altitude (up and down) and azimuth (side to side). However, since the heavenly bodies change continuously in altitude and azimuth as they arc through the sky this kind of mounting makes extended observation of an object difficult. That is why the *equatorial* mounting is preferred for astronomical work.

Once a telescope is properly set up on an equatorial mounting it can be easily moved to follow the stars. As before, the mounting has two axes at right angles to each other. One of these axes is adjusted so that it is parallel to the Earth's axis or, in other words,

points towards the celestial pole. It is called the polar axis. It makes an angle with the horizontal equal to the observer's latitude.

The path of a star, which describes a circle around the celestial pole, can then be followed simply by rotating the telescope around the polar axis. The telescope is thus scanning in right ascension, one of the co-ordinates of the grid system for locating heavenly bodies (see page 22). The second axis of the equatorial mounting is at right angles to the polar axis and thus allows the telescope to scan in declination, the other main celestial co-ordinate.

When a telescope is correctly set up and the local sidereal time is known, any star can be found by adjusting the telescope in right ascension and declination. To facilitate this, telescopes are often fitted with right ascension and declination setting circles, which once set enable objects to be located quickly.

117

Invisible Astronomy

Stars radiate energy, not only at the wavelengths of visible light, but also at the other wavelengths of the electromagnetic spectrum. This spectrum ranges from very short wavelength gamma-rays; through X-rays, ultraviolet rays, visible light rays and infrared rays; to long wavelength radio waves. The amount of radiation emitted at a particular wavelength varies from source to source. In other words, the source's brightness in the heavens depends on the wavelength at which you view it. The study of heavenly bodies at wavelengths other than visible light is known as invisible astronomy.

A major difficulty with invisible astronomy is the Earth's atmosphere. It is only transparent, in the invisible spectrum, to radio waves. So only radio wavelengths can be investigated from the ground. To observe the heavens at other invisible wavelengths, astronomers must send instruments above the atmosphere in rockets and spacecraft. Both ground-based radio astronomy and satellite astronomy have made spectacular discoveries, revealing a much more mysterious universe than was once suspected. Some of the strange bodies discovered by 'invisible' techniques are described opposite.

Karl Jansky pioneered radio astronomy in 1931 when he discovered radio noise coming from the Milky Way. Since then it has grown into one of the most fascinating branches of astronomy. The radio 'telescopes' astronomers use to gather radio waves from the cosmos have to be vast, since the signals are very weak. The dish type uses a parabolic reflector to gather the rays. The largest is the 305-metre (1000-ft) Arecibo (Puerto Rico) telescope located in a natural bowl in the ground. The largest fully steerable dish is the 100-metre (330-ft) Effelsberg telescope in Germany. Other radio telescopes use either several small dishes which work in concert, or criss-cross grids of long aerials. The most powerful radio telescope in the world is the Very Large Array in New Mexico, with 27 dishes on mobile tracks covering about 400 square kilometres.

Radio telescopes can also be operated in a radar mode, sending out radio pulses and detecting their echoes. Radar astronomy has been used to study meteors, the Moon and the planets, revealing, for example, that Venus has a retrograde rotation. Using radar, the Magellan Venus orbiter has resolved details on Venus only 120 metres across.

STRANGE MEMBERS OF THE UNIVERSE

Black hole The final stage in the collapse of a massive star. Stars like the Sun will eventually expand to become a red giant and then collapse, eventually turning into a white dwarf, a body not much bigger than the Earth. Stars tens of times more massive than the Sun will collapse catastrophically, probably after a supernova explosion, and form an unbelievably dense body whose gravity is so intense that not even light waves can escape from it. All external evidence of its presence disappears – it becomes a black hole. The presence of a black hole can, however, be inferred when it forms part of a binary star system. It will suck in material from the other star with such force that that material emits X-rays. Such rays have been detected from a source in Cygnus (Cyg X-1). Some astronomers believe that there could be 10 million black holes in our galaxy alone. Some astronomers have suggested that black holes may eventually swallow up all the matter in the universe.

Burster The name given to a type of X-ray star that erratically unleashes rapid bursts of X-radiation like machine-gun fire. These stars flare up in under a second and die down in less than a minute, sometimes emitting during this time 100,000 times the power of our Sun.

Pulsar A stellar body that emits its energy not continuously but in rapid pulses. This pulsing may be observed at visible or invisible wavelengths. Best known of the pulsars is the Crab pulsar, located in the Crab Nebula, which pulses 30 times a second. It is 'off' 97% of the time, each pulse lasting only 33 milliseconds. The Crab Nebula is known to be the remnants of a supernova explosion observed by Chinese astronomers in 1054, and pulsars appear to be born in supernovae. After the explosion of a massive star, the matter that was not ejected collapses to form a small, rapidly rotating object made up of neutrons packed tightly together. This so-called neutron star has a typical diameter of only about 16 km (10 mi). Its density is so great that a tablespoonful would weigh 1000 million tonnes.

Quasar Or quasi-stellar radio source: a body that looks like an ordinary star when viewed through the optical telescope, but which emits enormous energy at radio wavelengths. Quasars may be as small as 100 light-days across, whereas galaxies are of the order of 100,000 light-years across. Yet these quasars appear to be tens of times brighter than whole galaxies. Their spectra exhibit large red shifts (see page 62), which places them at enormous distances. The farthest ones are the remotest objects yet found, lying at least 10,000 million light-years away

Glossary of Terms

Aberration (1) Apparent displacement of star's position due to Earth's movement. (2) Distortion in optical instruments.

Absorption spectrum Stellar spectrum with dark lines caused by absorption in stellar atmosphere.

Albedo Reflecting power.

Altazimuth Telescope mounting allowing movement in both altitude and azimuth.

Aphelion Point in planet's orbit farthest from Sun.

Apogee Point in Moon's orbit farthest from Earth.

Astrology Pseudo-science that links human destiny with the relative positions of the heavenly bodies.

Astronomical unit Distance from Earth to Sun – 149,600,000 km (93,000,000 miles).

Azimuth Astronomical co-ordinate on horizon system. The angle between the great circle through the star and the zenith, and the meridian, measured west from the south point.

Barycentre Centre of mass, particularly of two mutually orbiting bodies.

Binary Star with two components.

Bolide Brilliant meteor.

Chromatic aberration Colour distortion produced by lens.

Chromosphere The lower part of Sun's atmosphere.

Coma Head of comet.

Comes Fainter component of binary.

Conjunction Term that applies when a planet, Earth and Sun are in line. A superior planet is in conjunction when it lies beyond Sun. An inferior planet is in superior conjunction when it lies beyond Sun, and is in inferior conjunction when it lies between Earth and Sun.

Constellation Group of stars.

Corona Outer atmosphere of Sun.

Cosmic rays Particle radiation from outer space.

Cosmogony Study of origin of the universe.

Counterglow See Gegenschein.

Declination Angular distance N or S from celestial equator.

Diurnal motion Apparent movement of stars due to Earth's rotation.

Doppler effect Apparent change in wavelength of a star's light due to its motion towards or away from observer.

Eclipse Passage of one body in front of another, blotting out its light.

Ecliptic Apparent path of Sun around celestial sphere.

Elongation Angular distance of an inferior planet from Sun.

Emission spectrum Bright-line spectrum produced by incandescent gas.

Equator, celestial Projection of Earth's equator on celestial sphere.

Equinox Time of equal night and day when Sun appears directly above the equator. Point of intersection of ecliptic and celestial equator.

First Point of Aries Point at which Sun crosses equator moving north. The zero point for measurement of right ascension.

Galaxy Star system. The Galaxy refers to the system to which the Sun belongs.

Gegenschein Faint glow in night sky opposite to Sun.

Gibbous Phase of Moon or planet when more than half of its surface is illuminated.

Hertzsprung-Russell diagram Graph that related a star's brightness and spectrum.

Inferior planet One whose orbit is smaller than the Earth's.

Libration Irregularities in Moon's motion.

Light-year Distance light travels in a year – about 10 million million km, (6 million million miles).

Magnetosphere Magnetic envelope around Earth.

Magnitude (1) Apparent – the brightness of a body as it appears to an observer on Earth. (2) Absolute – the brightness as it would appear from a distance of 10 parsecs (32.6 light-years).

Main sequence Band on the Hertzsprung-Russell diagram in which most stars lie.

Meridian Great circle passing through zenith and N and S celestial poles.

Nadir Point on celestial sphere diametrically opposite zenith.

Nutation Slight nodding of Earth's axis due to influence of Moon.

Occultation Eclipse of one celestial body by another.

Opposition Position of superior planet when it is in line with Sun and Earth, with the Earth in between.

Parallax Apparent movement of a body against a background when viewed from different directions.

Parsec Distance at which a body would show parallax of 1 second of arc; equals 3·26 light-years.

Penumbra Region of partial shadow in an eclipse or sunspot.

Perigee Closest point to Earth in Moon's orbit.

Perihelion Closest point to Sun in planet's orbit.

Perturbation Disturbance in a body's orbit due to gravitational attraction of another.

Phases Apparent change in shape of planet or Moon due to different areas being illuminated by Sun.

Photosphere Visible surface of Sun.

Plasma Gas of ionized atoms.

Populations I and II Classes of stars: I are young, II are old.

Precession Slow circular motion of Earth's axis in space.

Prominence Fountain of fiery gas rising from Sun's surface.

Proper motion Motion of star across the line of sight.

Quadrature Position of Moon or planet at right angles to the Sun, as seen from the Earth.

Radial motion Motion of star toward or away from us.

Radiant Point from which a meteor shower appears to originate.

Red shift Shift in spectral lines of starlight towards the red, due to Doppler effect.

Retrograde motion Motion in a direction opposite from usual.

Right ascension Astronomical co-ordinate equivalent to terrestrial longitude. The angular distance measured eastwards from the First Point of Aries, expressed in hours, minutes and seconds of sidereal time.

Saros Cycle of 18 years 11 days after which eclipses of Sun and Moon occur in the same order in the same time.

Satellite Small body that revolves around a planet.

Selenography Study of the Moon.

Shooting star Meteor.

Sidereal Relating to the stars: (1) sidereal period: time it takes Moon or planet to circle round primary body and return to same place with respect to the stars. (2) sidereal time: time based on rotation of Earth with respect to stars. Sidereal day is 23 hr 56 min 4 sec long.

Solar time Local time by Sun.

Solar wind Stream of particles coming from Sun.

Solstice Time when Sun appears farthest north or south of celestial equator.

Spherical aberration Poor definition caused by incorrect curvature of a telescope lens or mirror.

Supergiant Huge luminous star typically hundreds of times bigger than Sun.

Superior planet One whose orbit is larger than the Earth's.

Supernova Exploding star of great brilliance.

Synodic period Time between when Moon or planet presents the same appearance in the heavens: eg synodic period – the time it takes Moon to complete its phases ($29\frac{1}{2}$ days).

Syzygy Occasion when three bodies, eg Sun, Moon and Earth, are in line in space, as at new or full moon.

Terminator Line dividing lit and unlit regions of illuminated body.

Transit Passage of (1) star across meridian, or (2) smaller body across the face of another, eg inferior planet across disc of Sun.

Umbra Central dark region of (1) sunspot, or (2) shadow during an eclipse.

Universe All that exists: space, and the matter – stars, Sun, Moon, planets – and energy within it.

Van Allen belts Regions of intense radiation around Earth where charged particles have become trapped by Earth's magnetic field.

White dwarf Small ultra-dense dying star.

Zenith Point on celestial sphere directly above observer.

Zodiac Belt of 12 constellations along ecliptic, through which Sun, Moon and planets appear to move.

Zodiacal light Faint cone-shaped glow along the ecliptic often seen at dawn or dusk. Caused by reflection of sunlight by meteoric dust in plane of ecliptic.

Index

ACKNOWLEDGEMENTS

The authors and publishers wish to thank the following for their help in supplying photographs for this book on the pages indicated:

American Meteorite Laboratory 106 bottom, 107 bottom; Anglo-Australian Observatory 116; Californian Institute of Technology 8, 42, 52, 53, 54 bottom, 55, 56, 57, 59, 60, 61, 62 top, 67, 68, 70 top, 86 centre, 92 top, 96, 97 bottom, 100 bottom, 101 bottom, 103, 104 left, 105 bottom; Institute of Geological Sciences 88 right; Robin Kerrod 8 (inset), 13, 18, 20, 64 centre, 90 top, 97 top left, 107 top, 108 top, 112 (insets), 113, 115 bottom, 117; NASA 70 bottom, 71 bottom, 72, 76, 79, 81, 87 top, 88 left, 93, 97 top right, 102, 108 bottom, 110 right, 112; Novosti 87 bottom; Ronan Picture Library 64 top, 106 top; Royal Astronomical Society 12; Science Museum (Crown Copyright) 10; United States Naval Observatory 54 top, 58, 62 bottom, 104 top right; University of Michigan 46; ZEFA 118; Christian Veillet 100 top, 101 centre.

Picture research by Jackie Cookson and Penny Warn